D0024364

BFI TV Classics

BFI TV Classics is a series of books celebrating key individual television programmes and series. Television scholars, critics and novelists provide critical readings underpinned with careful research, alongside a personal response to the programme and a case for its 'classic' status.

Also Published:

Buffy the Vampire Slayer
Anne Billson

Doctor Who
Kim Newman

Edge of Darkness
John Caughie

The Likely Lads
Phil Wickham

The Office
Ben Walters

Our Friends in the North
Michael Eaton

Queer as Folk
Glyn Davis

Seinfeld
Nicholas Mirzoeff

Seven Up
Stella Bruzzi

The Singing Detective
Glen Creeber

Star Trek

Ina Rae Hark

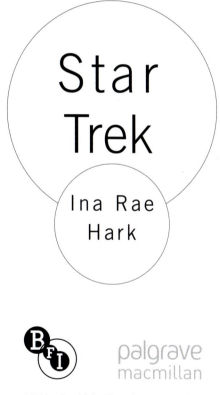

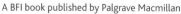

A BFI book published by Palgrave Macmillan

First published in 2008 by
PALGRAVE MACMILLAN
Houndmills, Basingstoke, Hampshire RG21 6XS and
175 Fifth Avenue, New York, N.Y. 10010
Companies and Representatives throughout the world

on behalf of the

BRITISH FILM INSTITUTE
21 Stephen Street, London W1T 1LN
www.bfi.org.uk

There's more to discover about film and television through the BFI. Our
world-renowned archive, cinemas, festivals, films, publications and learning
resources are here to inspire you.

PALGRAVE MACMILLAN is the global academic imprint of the Palgrave Macmillan
division of St. Martin's Press, LLC and of Palgrave Macmillan Ltd.
Macmillan® is a registered trademark in the United States, United Kingdom
and other countries. Palgrave is a registered trademark in the European
Union and other countries.

Images from *Star Trek*, Desilu Productions/Norway Corporation/Paramount Television;
Star Trek: The Next Generation, Paramount Television; *Star Trek: Deep Space Nine*,
Paramount Television; *Star Trek: Voyager*, Paramount Pictures/United Paramount Network;
Enterprise, Paramount Pictures/Braga Productions/Rick Berman Productions.

Whilst considerable effort has been made to correctly identify the copyright holders, this has
not been possible in all cases. We apologise for any omissions or mistakes in the credits and
we will endeavour to remedy, in future editions, errors brought to our attention by the
relevant rights holder.

None of the content of this publication is intended to imply that it is endorsed by the
programme's broadcaster or production companies involved.

Set by Cambrian Typesetters, Camberley, Surrey
Printed in China

This book is printed on paper suitable for recycling and made from fully
managed and sustained forest sources. Logging, pulping and manufacturing
processes are expected to conform to the environmental regulations of the
country of origin.

British Library Cataloguing-in-Publication Data
A catalogue record for this book is available from the British Library

ISBN 978-1-84457-214-4

Contents

To Sharon, my sister of the heart.

And to Gene L. Coon and Michael Piller, the unsung helmsmen of the best of *Trek*, both beamed up far too soon.

Acknowledgments

I've been discussing *Trek* with anyone who would listen for forty years now, so there are many people who have helped me form the ideas contained in this volume. First and foremost I thank Sharon Kirkland for her always brilliant insights that made me look at the *Trek* universe in exciting new ways (and I thank *Deep Space Nine* for allowing us to connect with one another). Of the many others with whom I've talked *Trek*, particular thanks go to Karen Robinson Kern, Donald Fulton, David Hill, Jeanne Carriere, Ray Cosner, Jean Lisette Aroeste, Joel Myerson, Greta Little, Rhonda Wilcox, Brett Cox, Mark Jancovich, Amy Villarejo, Matthew Tinkom, Susan Vanderborg, Daniel Bernardi, Roberta Pearson, Marguerite Krause, Una McCormack and Merrie Kapp. Beyond 'real life' I have benefited from the give and take in several online *Trek* communities: RAFL, andytalk, garakbashir, 9anon, psiphi, trekweb, the SlipstreamBBS and ExIsle.

I have been privileged to have some one-on-one exchanges with various creative personnel who worked on the *Trek* shows and take the opportunity here to express my gratitude to Andrew J. Robinson, Armin Shimerman, Robert Hewitt Wolfe and, especially, René Auberjonois for his generosity and kindness for many years.

At the BFI I am indebted to my longtime editor Rebecca Barden for asking me to write this book and to her colleagues Julian Grainger and Sophia Contento. Thanks also to copyeditor Joy Tucker and Steve Redwood at Palgrave Macmillan.

As always, the support and advice from Steven Cohan have been invaluable, even if *Star Trek* is one of the few things I know more about than he does.

Trekker's Log, Stardate 1908200.7

On Thursday, 8 September 1966, at 8.30pm, *Star Trek* premiered. I did
not tune in. That Friday Mr Fulton, my high school senior physics
teacher, started class with an enthusiastic discourse on how the
programme treated actual physics. Intrigued, and with positive
impressions of William Shatner and DeForest Kelley from previous
television roles, I tuned in the next week. The episode was 'Charlie X'
and I wasn't impressed. I knew too many annoying guys like that at
school, even if they didn't have the power to make things happen by
pure thought (thank goodness!) I switched off midway through and
watched *Bewitched* (ABC 1964–72). But physics class continued to
revolve around *Trek* discussion every Friday, and I felt left out. On 20
October, I decided to skip *Bewitched*, so I sat down and watched the
seventh episode, 'What Are Little Girls Made Of?' in its entirety. The
rest, as they say, is history.

The storyline concerned Roger Korby (Michael Strong), a
brilliant scientist believed lost on a mission. He had survived, however,
and had perfected a process by which a human's entire consciousness
could be transferred to an immortal android body. The central debate
concerned whether this would be a boon to humankind or a terrible
mistake. To me it was, as Mr Spock (Leonard Nimoy) would say,
fascinating, and I wasn't sure the answer given, that the essence of
humanity was inseparable from our perishable shells of flesh and blood,

Roger Korby and Andrea

was convincing. The revelation that Korby himself was an android completely shocked me, novice to the conventions of science fiction that I was then, but it seemed that his inability to articulate his humanness in anything but theorems and equations was offset by the pure AI Andrea's (Sherry Jackson) obvious and sincere love for him. I didn't know how to take it when Korby immolated both of them, but I knew that regular old television never made me think this hard or feel this confused. I was also intrigued that Kirk (William Shatner) knew he could alert his half-Vulcan first officer to the fact that a duplicate was impersonating him by planting a racial slur in the duplicate's conversational repertoire. How wonderful to have an expression of prejudice seem so out of place, even if the coda showed that Spock was a bit hurt that Kirk could even frame such a crude insult as 'I'm sick of your half-breed interference.'

From then on, *Trek* was my obsession. I carried it with me to college, watching seasons two and three in dorm TV lounges where you could find everyone from an heiress to the Bayer pharmaceuticals family to a black power activist who would go on to be a famous Civil Rights attorney. A friend from those days told a mutual acquaintance of mine decades later, 'Ina was a Trekkie before they had a name for them.'

For the next twenty years I did all the fannish things any self-respecting Trekkie would do. I wrote a letter in the famous campaign to get the show a third season. I rewatched syndicated reruns over and over, until the video age dawned and I could actually own the episodes. I attended *Trek* conventions, subscribed to fan club newsletters, wrote fanfiction. I didn't ever dress up as a Klingon, but I possess a formidable collection of *Trek* T-shirts. Of course I was thrilled when *Star Trek* came back to life, at first in the animated version and then the films. When a spinoff series with a new crew was announced, I was wary but enthusiastic. While I grew to admire *The Next Generation* (*TNG*), I never really *liked* it. The emotional stakes that were always so high for Kirk, Spock and McCoy (DeForest Kelley) were absent. The crew seemed more facilitators for the plots than drivers of them and too many conflicts had as the opponent some spatial phenomenon whose motives didn't have any of the troubling ambiguity of Roger Korby's. And there were only so many times I could stand to hear discussions of remodulating the shield harmonics or reconfiguring the deflector to emit a tachyon burst.

I had resigned myself to the fact that lightning doesn't strike twice, and I wasn't going to get as carried away with new *Trek* as I had when I was a teenager. Then *Deep Space Nine* (*DS9*) debuted and I was in love all over again. The most talented acting ensemble ever to be gathered for a *Trek* show portrayed a wounded and emotionally scarred bunch of humans and aliens whose progress towards community and shared goals was a lot more thrilling than watching those consummate professionals on *TNG*. *DS9* and the internet came along at roughly the same time, and my engagement with fandom, which had waned over the years, was also re-energised by this new way of communicating with other Trekkers (as we 'serious' aficionados now called ourselves).

I followed *Voyager* and *Enterprise* because I was so deeply en-Trekked that I was going to watch the television franchise no matter

3

Captain Kathryn Janeway

where it led, but I was not at all happy where these last incarnations not so boldly went. *Voyager*, on an episode-by-episode basis, could come up with stories to equal the best of the other series, especially meditations on difficult ethical issues like 'Jetrel', 'Distant Origin', 'Nothing Human', 'Living Witness' and 'Flesh and Blood'. The disconnect between the situation in which the stranded crew found itself and the actions they took (and the incredibly lucky consequences of those actions) was, however, too wide for me to deal with. Moreover, due partly to Kate Mulgrew's mannered performance and partly to writers who couldn't figure out how to portray a woman as a moral touchstone, Janeway drove me absolutely crazy. She usually came off as a scold rather than an ethical exemplar, at best like a combination of your most inspirational university philosophy professor and the stern but loving parent who always made you eat your vegetables, at worst like one of those caricatured spinster librarians telling unruly patrons to hush in pre-feminist discourse.[1] *Enterprise*, the supposed new beginning, was never more than tired repetition of ideas executed better in other *Trek*s, as if I were watching reruns. As Jan Johnson-Smith has observed: '*Enterprise* shows space as the final frontier, but it relies upon anachronistic "old frontier" ideologies in much of its approach, a sad comment upon *Star Trek*'s overall ideological direction.'[2]

Broadcast television lives by advertising revenue, and advertisers prize the eighteen to forty-nine demographic. It has been said that if demographics had mattered when the original series was on, it wouldn't have been cancelled so soon. My history of watching and enjoying *Trek* matches up uncannily with entrance into and departure from that demographic. I was seventeen when *Star Trek* premiered and forty-nine when *DS9* ended and *Voyager* completed its best season, the fifth. To some extent *Trek* is, I believe, my generation's myth, and as the demographic moved on from being dominated by us Cold War-raised baby-boomers to a critical mass of the much more wary and cynical Gen Xers, the franchise found itself drifting. An exchange in a *Voyager* episode, 'Future's End', which had the crew whisked back in time to 1996, pinpoints the difficulty. Chakotay (Robert Beltran) and Torres (Roxann Dawson) are captured by a survivalist militia whose members hate 'the Feds', whom they believe have sent the newcomers: 'There are two forces at work in the world. The drive toward collectivity and the drive toward individuality,' their captor explains. 'You are the former, and I am the latter.' The right here co-opts *Trek*'s sacred mantra of individualism, deemed incompatible with the big government liberal humanism that also underscores the *Trek* ideology. We Great Society-boomers still believed that a perfected government could ensure the best environment for realising the individual. Post-Reagan, that belief collapsed for the younger audience.

While I bring to a critique of *Trek* the enthusiasms of a fan who sequentially experienced each incarnation in its historical context, as it was first broadcast, I also very early on approached *Trek* with the analytical eye of the textual scholar I would become. The original series was the subject of a senior thesis in college and one of my first academic publications as a university professor, and I continued to write and present on the franchise when it revived in the late 1980s. Rewatching more than 700 hours of *Trek* for this volume allows me to make connections that may not have been apparent without the whole *Trek* television text before me.

Much has already been written about *Star Trek*, but often its goal is to speculate on what *Star Trek* tells us about something else: about physics, metaphysics or ethics, about American cultural mythology, about how the programme naturalises sexism, racism or hegemonic global capitalism within a utopian vision of the future. I was never so naive as to think that a show produced and marketed by a vast multimedia entertainment conglomerate would instead adhere to the ideologies of NOW, Amnesty International or Greenpeace, so the indignation that fuelled much of the cultural studies take on *Trek* during the 1990s never animated me. Nor was I one of those fans who looked to *Trek* as a consolation when my life was difficult or as a blueprint for building a better world. Indeed, it was those times that *Trek* underlined how tenuous social progress could be, how easy it is to relapse into prejudice and hatred, which made the deepest impression upon me. Hokey as it was, I never forgot the ending of the original series episode 'Let That Be Your Last Battlefield'. It's the one in which aliens who are literally white on one side and black on the other have fallen into intractable race hatred over who is black on the left side and who on the right. When the last two survivors return to their home planet to discover that the warring sides have completely annihilated each other, do they wake up and make peace? Nope, they beam down and continue their efforts to destroy each other. When Uhura (Nichelle Nichols) asks if hate was all they ever had, Kirk responds that it wasn't, but that it's all they have left – words as pertinent to the current world situation as to the Watts riots that inspired the episode.

What I have always loved most in *Star Trek* is what attracted me to other favourite genres, like World War II platoon and submarine sagas and Westerns set in Dodge City or Deadwood: stories of disparate, distrustful, culturally alienated and emotionally wounded people who somehow come together for the common good when the chips are down. This commentary will be about how *Trek*'s forty-year narrative encompassed a galaxy full of such people, their conflicts and their epiphanies of connection. Since the original series is the true television classic, the one that made cultural icons of Kirk and Spock, taught generations about Klingons, warp speed, beaming up and raising shields, inspired the look of mobile phones, PDAs and floppy disks, and provided the template for most of the manifestations of media fandom, it receives the longest and most detailed analysis. The spinoffs get their due as well because the return of the *Trek* universe to television after twenty years, a return that encompassed twenty-five seasons of four additional series, is also an impressive achievement in that medium. While not dismissive of or uninformed by historical, cultural and ideological contexts, what follows is first and foremost about, well, *Star Trek*.

Ina Rae Hark
19 August 2007
My birthday, and Gene Roddenberry's

1 Course Plotted and Laid In

I'd say that at its heart, *Star Trek*, especially the original series, is a romantic adventure which appeals to the dreamer in all of us. It says that there's a better future waiting for us all, one where humanity can pursue its best intentions. It's idealistic, sexy and fun. Who wouldn't want to be a crew member on the original *Enterprise*? Later *Trek*s either attempted to recapture that spirit (*TNG, Enterprise*) or reimagine it in the context of the worldview of our current times (*DS9, Voyager*).

Robert Hewitt Wolfe, staff writer on *Star Trek: Deep Space Nine*[3]

The parameters of what would become the *Trek* universe developed out of a number of choices made about the premise for the original series. Roddenberry pitched it to the Desilu production company as '*Wagon Train* to the stars', probably because the lengthiest part of his CV as a television writer consisted of scripts for Westerns, including twenty-four episodes of *Have Gun, Will Travel* (CBS 1957–63). There is no reason that this could not have been a viable premise for a science-fiction series set in the future in space: a large transport ship drops off groups of colonists at a wide variety of alien worlds, focusing on some particular issue for each group per episode or encountering external threats that endanger the ship. This was, however, not at all the type of series whose outline Roddenberry had registered with the Writers' Guild in 1964.

Star Trek's iconic crew

9

Roddenberry's concept drew on the other half of his CV and even more on his own personal experience prior to becoming a television writer. The son and brother of career police officers, he served with the LAPD from 1949 through 1956. Many of his early teleplays were for crime programmes such as *Mr District Attorney* (ABC/Ziv 1951–4), *Highway Patrol* (Ziv 1955–9), *Naked City* (ABC 1958–63), *The Detectives* (ABC/NBC 1959–62) and *I Led Three Lives* (Ziv 1953–6). Roddenberry had also served in World War II, and two of the pre-*Star Trek* series with which he had the most extensive involvement concerned the military: *The West Point Story* (CBS 1956–8) and his first project as writer-producer to get a network pick-up, *The Lieutenant* (Arena 1963–4). Prior to his success with *The Lieutenant*, Roddenberry had written an unsold pilot for a series set in the Pacific during the war, *APO 923*. *Star Trek*, about a group of people in uniform who were sworn to serve and protect others, fitted well within this range of its creator's expertise. Specifically, Starfleet was the military arm of the United Federation of Planets, the *Enterprise* one of its capital ships, with its personnel holding various ranks that paralleled those in the United States Navy. For the crew, space was less 'the final frontier' than the farthest ocean.[4]

Situating the regular characters and their vessel within a military hierarchy provided reasons for the *Enterprise* to go from strange new world to strange new world on its mission, avoiding either the always-deferred closure of odyssey series like *Lost in Space* (CBS 1965–8), *Battlestar Galactica* (Universal 1978, 1980) or *Space: 1999* (ITC 1975–7) (or *Trek*'s later *Voyager*), in which the goal was to return to an old or find a new home, or the aimlessness that might have pervaded a series about pure, undirected exploration (a lesson the creators of *Enterprise* were slow to learn). The opening narration may define as the prime mission for the ship 'to explore strange new worlds, to seek out new life and new civilisations, to boldly go where no man has gone before'; a discarded earlier version is more accurate (if less evocative): 'Assigned a five-year patrol of our galaxy, the giant starship visits Earth colonies, regulates commerce, and explores strange new worlds and new civilisations.'[5] To be sure, the premise also required the *Enterprise* to serve a myriad of functions that would doubtless have been assigned to many different types of vessels in a real space navy. It functioned as a heavily armed warship summoned to deal with enemy incursions, routinely answered distress calls, conducted medical examinations on human colonies, transported supplies and passengers, and negotiated mining rights. Occasionally it mapped an uncharted area of space or made first contact with the inhabitants of a planet, but these missions were in the minority. And the ship rarely went voluntarily where no human had gone before, although it did repeatedly return to sites of initial human failure. The *Enterprise* served as the equivalent to twentieth-century vessels, from aircraft carrier to C31 transport to Coast Guard cutter. Combined with the occasions when previously unknown entities came from unexplored regions to give our galaxy a hostile look-over, the ship's multitasking provided the show with sufficient different situations to engage the crew in dramatic conflict over its seventy-nine episodes.

The *Enterprise* had a crew of over 400, and the duties and functions of those chosen to be regular or recurring characters among them were an initial signifier of the deepest concerns of the series, as they would be on the succeeding *Trek*s as well. One choice made by the producers was to divide the specialities represented into three broad categorisations, denoted by the colours of their tunics.[6] The captain, helmsman and navigator wore gold. It denoted command officers, those who directed the course of the ship and deployed its assets, such as phasers, photon torpedoes and tractor beams. Blue was the colour of the science specialists, including the medical staff. Although Spock served as both the ship's science officer and its first officer, his primary allegiance to enquiry and research was indicated by the fact that his tunic was blue and not gold. If the blues gathered and analysed data for the golds to base command decisions upon, everything that allowed the ship to do what it was commanded to do fell to the hands-on crew in red, who kept the engines and ship's systems humming, enabled communications, performed secretarial duties and provided security. (These duties would be grouped under the rubric of 'operations' in *TNG* and the colours for command and operations would be reversed in the twenty-fourth-century spinoffs.)

Having come up with a workable, narrative-generating premise for a space-based series, one that would underlie the subsequent *Trek* starship shows, Roddenberry and his staff were still faced by some of the particular demands of such a premise. Since each episode was to take the *Enterprise* to a different planet or area of space, a dramatic problem had to be posed, dealt with and left behind every episode. Television series about crime-solving and the law or about doctors have always dominated the ranks of hour-long dramas because they come with a built-in narrative formula. The problem (the crime, the case, the disease) comes to the protagonists and the story reaches a natural conclusion when the criminal is apprehended, the jury's decision comes in, or the patient either recovers or dies. *Star Trek* eventually came up with a formula to give its plots a sense of urgency and excitement, but it was a formula that frequently derailed more complex problem-solving approaches by the crew to the new life and new civilisations they encountered. Nearly every episode

11

reveals that some aspect of these new persons, creatures or phenomena poses a clear and present danger to a regular character, to the *Enterprise* itself, and/or to densely populated planets and solar systems. Often the jeopardy is on the clock: so many hours remain before the ship's orbit will decay, or the mysterious disease will claim its final victim, or the dangerous entity who has taken over will reach the inhabited system it wishes to destroy. Scripts would engage seriously to a certain point on whether a particular culture very different from that of Earth should be interfered with, whether a radically different life form's ideology should be respected. Again and again, trumping the debate, only one course of action will save the ship, the endangered crew members, or the galaxy.

On the other hand, as in the real-life drama of *Apollo 13* that would occur less than a year after *Star Trek* was cancelled, this format showcased the resourcefulness and ingenuity of the crew. It also foregrounded those principles they held so firmly that they would not compromise them in the face of imminent death. *Star Trek*'s appeal

Captain James T. Kirk

First Officer Spock

13

always derived from its people more than its plots. Therefore, whether the jeopardy scenarios employed imaginative science-fiction concepts ('The Devil in the Dark'), insight into topical issues ('A Taste of Armageddon') and wrenching moral conundrums ('The City on the Edge of Forever') or silly premises ('Spock's Brain') and high camp ('The Gamesters of Triskelion'), they were equally designed to allow the characters and their relationships centre stage.

The captain was understandably at the centre of the action, but no *Trek* captain would ever again be so central as James T. Kirk. Although Spock or McCoy have their own personal stories to act out as part of the larger action plot in some episodes, it is usually Kirk who overcomes the obstacle that threatens the crew, ship or mission. In a quite unmilitary fashion that was addressed head-on and altered in the first season of *TNG*, Kirk beams down on nearly every away mission. Just as he commands the *Enterprise*, so he directs the unfolding plots of nearly all the episodes. As the only other character whose actor was contracted to appear in all the season one episodes, Spock's role as first officer/science officer and foil/buddy to Kirk retains the dynamic of the rejected first pilot, 'The Cage'. In the original version, the first officer, 'Number One' (Majel Barrett), was emotionally repressed, the butt of comparisons to a computer and the captain's Other by virtue of being a woman. When the network had doubts about a female second-in-command, especially when played by a little-known actress who was his mistress, Roddenberry merged the emotional repression with the Otherness of the pilot's alien but vaguely characterised junior officer Spock. In later series the first officer's role was to run interference for the captain and to serve as a sounding board for command decisions, but Spock's scientific acumen, his ability to supply needed information and analysis, constitutes his primary function on the *Enterprise*. Kirk's confidant was not one of his subordinate line officers but the ship's surgeon, Dr Leonard McCoy. These three characters far overshadowed the rest of the senior staff: chief engineer Scott (James Doohan),

14

Dr Leonard McCoy

helmsman Sulu (George Takei), communications officer Uhura and, later, navigator and weapons officer Chekov (Walter Koenig).

These character templates remained in the spinoff series but some roles were de-emphasised and others enhanced, although the captain–first officer dyad always figured strongly. No medical officer was ever as central as McCoy, although *Voyager*'s Emergency Medical Hologram (Robert Picardo) came close. That show's Tom Paris (Robert Duncan McNeill) got the most screen time of any helmsman/pilot. *Enterprise*'s engineer Trip Tucker (Connor Trinneer) equalled First Officer T'Pol (Jolene Blalock) in importance. The communications officer, on the other hand, disappeared as a self-contained assignment until *Enterprise* and Hoshi Sato (Linda Park) rarely transcended the 'hailing frequencies open' function of Uhura. New specialities emerged as well. Security is a major duty of later series' regulars such as *TNG*'s Worf (Michael Dorn), *DS9*'s Odo (René Auberjonois), *Voyager*'s Tuvok (Tim Russ) and *Enterprise*'s Reed (Dominic Keating), but so undervalued in *Star Trek* that it was left to the ignominious 'redshirts', famous for their fatal inability to secure much of anything. Civilian purveyors of hospitality came onboard with recurring bartender Guinan (Whoopi Goldberg) in *TNG* and regulars Quark (Armin Shimerman) and Neelix (Ethan Phillips) in *DS9* and *Voyager*.

15

Star Trek's ensemble is renowned for its ground-breaking diversity, and such multicultural, multiracial casting would be a trademark of all the series. The first three spinoffs undertook this mission almost programmatically in regard to three significant character functions. The captain's chair became the place in which to stress human gender and ethnic diversity. Jon Wagner and Jan Lundeen note that 'Captain Kirk, the prototypical *Star Trek* hero, is the ultimate "neutral" human: a white Midwestern [American] middle-class male.'[7] Succeeding him were a white European male, an African-American male and a white American woman. In each case, only one Kirkian trait was altered at a time – we never saw a female from Shanghai in command, for instance – but the human ensembles in lesser ranks did broaden the differing combinations of race, gender and national origin.

Each of these series also maintained the pattern of having one regular whose Otherness was more marked and who served as the outsider looking in, as Spock had done. These successive outsiders differ not just from humans but from alien humanoids. *TNG*'s Data (Brent Spiner) is an inorganic android. *DS9*'s Odo is an organic but from a species of shape-shifters whose default gelatinous state can morph into anything from a briefcase to a bar stool, a German shepherd to a duplicate of a Starfleet admiral. *Voyager*'s Doctor is a 'photonic' being more human in appearance and culture than any of the others but, as a projected computer program, not only inorganic but immaterial. He is joined later in the series by another outlier, the human cyborg Seven of Nine (Jeri Ryan).

A third regular cast slot in *TNG*, *DS9* and *Voyager* is dedicated to a member of an alien species that in the prior series served as an antagonist to the Federation. This allows for greater understanding of that species' culture and motivations and stresses the *Trek* postulate that there are no permanent enemies. *TNG* introduced the Klingon Worf, *DS9* put a Ferengi on the station and had several recurring Cardassians, and Seven of Nine added a Borg to the onboard community of *Voyager*.

The prequel *Enterprise* retrenched, essentially returning to the paradigm of the original series. Once again there was a familiar 'big three': the white, male American captain, his Vulcan first officer T'Pol and his southern American good friend Trip Tucker. Humanoid aliens are as 'Other' as the regular ensemble gets. There are no prior foes to be welcomed into the fold of the starship crew, although the recurring character of Andorian captain Shran (Jeffrey Combs), an early adversary of Captain Jonathan Archer (Scott Bakula) who becomes his steadfast ally, somewhat fulfils that function. Whatever the failings of *Trek* to live up to its claims of complete racial tolerance and the decentring of patriarchy and Western hegemony, it is still the only space-based franchise to give women and minorities the lead role.[8] Many saw the back-pedalling of *Enterprise* as implying that twenty-first-century science-fiction viewers could not identify with a female or minority captain. It does say something about Trekkers that they resisted such a reactionary gesture; those fans who had melted away during *DS9* and *Voyager* did not miraculously reappear once Jonathan Archer took command.

This tracks with a core *Trek* theme. Every crew and its ancillary personnel represent the possibility of unity despite difference, although each ensemble points to an outer limit of difference beyond which tolerance but not total inclusion lies. Frequently defined as 'liberal humanist' in philosophy, *Trek*, on the macro-level, looks for a paradigm by which cultures ever more divergent can confederate, ally or at least coexist and, on the micro-level, works out the boundaries that define the 'human'. As Michèle and Duncan Barrett assert: 'In the colonial history of earth the trend is towards a restriction of who is deemed to be human; in *Star Trek* the issue is to "humanise" as many people as possible.'[9] When Kirk tells Spock in the sixth *Trek* film, *The Undiscovered Country* (Paramount 1991), that 'everybody's human', the statement at once reflects the American melting-pot ideal that no matter how diverse our origins we can, through shared values, become the same – and its less attractive converse, that anyone who is truly 'human' would want to share those values if given the opportunity. Conflating a welcoming inclusivity with the desire to assimilate the Other, the Federation's utopian ideologues don't ascribe much value to the life form that says 'Sorry, not interested' to the membership invitation. It's difficult to know whether there was intentional irony in giving the fearsome Borg, who are happy to incorporate any technologically valuable species into their 'collective', the mantra of 'Resistance is futile. You will be assimilated' upon their introduction in *TNG*; but the *DS9* writers fully appreciated it when they had a traitor to Starfleet declare that the Federation was 'worse than the Borg . . . they assimilate you and you don't even notice'.

17

This is the ultimate calumny regarding the Federation's position of moral superiority, for collectives like the Borg are the antithesis of what *Trek* conceives the ideal social organisation to be. As Thomas Richards observes, 'Star Trek values the individual at the expense of all groups', that 'individual action matters far more than

Picard assimilated by the Borg

divine or collective action'.[10] Yet the importance of an individuality never submerged in a larger whole does not negate the fact that only when these autonomous individuals voluntarily confederate is the ideal society within reach. This is the crucial distinction between the Borg and the Federation but also an area of intersection. In *Trek* 'no man is an island because every man is a continent', Richards says.[11] Untrammelled individualism leads to anarchy, but Starfleet is after all organised by rank, duty and the chain of command. Seven of Nine, the human liberated from the Borg, often insists without any sense of contradiction that she is now an individual *and* that the crew of *Voyager* are her 'new collective'. That she emphasises the transition from collective cog to individual as often as the transition from Borg drone to human being epitomises the *Trek* conflation of the two.

The following chapters will delineate how each series adopted very different preoccupations within these parameters of the *Trek* universe. Nevertheless, that universe does have fixed parameters. Starfleet crews live in a universe where time travel is possible, faster than light speeds standard, teleporting across considerable distances via molecular disassembly and reassembly commonplace, communication with other species via 'universal translators' routine. They operate under the Prime Directive of Non-Interference, designed to forestall imperialist ambitions. The present of the five series spans the years from 16 April 2151 (the first episode of *Enterprise*) to 2378, the year that *Voyager* returns to the Alpha Quadrant. Flashbacks and temporal adventures extend the characters' range back to the nineteenth century and forward to the thirty-first.

Missions frequently unfold according to tried and true tropes of science-fiction narratives. Every *Trek* series features at least one episode (and usually many more) that involve time travel; that involve telepathy; that involve the characters' bodies and minds being taken over by incorporeal beings; that involve characters being duplicated, twinned, split or sharing space with a displaced temporal self; and that serve as an allegory for social problems of the present. The three series set in the twenty-fourth century (*TNG*, *DS9* and *Voyager*) offer holographic environments for the crew members' recreation, and these environments can be relied upon to malfunction dangerously at one time or another.

Although the Federation is only in its embryonic stages in *Enterprise*, all the series posit that membership in a multiworld alliance devoted to exploration, colonisation and mutual protection is the best political structure for any species that is capable of deep space travel at 'warp speeds'. The Federation is never shown to be free of flaws, and it is regularly threatened by corruption, infiltration, treason and dictatorial leanings from without and from within. Nevertheless, and this is a key component of *Trek* in comparison with many other science-fiction universes, a 'big government' that works for the good is always seen as possible and ultimately the most equitable. There is limited sympathy for small, rebel factions within certain, historically specific situations, but a permanent oppositional stance, as seen in a *Firefly*

19

(FOX 2002–3) or *Farscape* (Sci Fi 1999–2003) – or their forebear, the British *Blake's Seven* (BBC 1978–81), whose tyrannical planetary coalition was not named the Federation by accident – is never portrayed as desirable. The often-cited *Trek* 'optimism' is not as naively blinkered as it is sometimes rendered, but *Trek*'s vision of peace proving better than war and enemies eventually becoming friends is definitely utopian in a genre that often tilts the other way.

2 *Star Trek*: This Side of Paradise

Star Trek went into formal development in 1964 as a commercial television series with Gene Roddenberry, Desilu, and NBC all hoping to make money from the project. It's important to understand that, first and foremost. *Star Trek* was not created or developed as a critical study of truth, life's fundamental principles, or concepts of reasoned doctrines. We just wanted a hit series.

Herb Solow, Desilu executive[12]

As the foundation upon which the whole *Trek* franchise was built, *Star Trek* has invariably been rewritten from the perspective of the succeeding 'modern *Treks*' as well as from the aggregate of fan discourses that have redefined it according to the needs it fulfilled for various *Trek* constituencies. It is necessary therefore to analyse *Star Trek* as the television show Gene Roddenberry sold to Desilu, which then sold it to NBC, only after CBS had decided it would rather fulfil its science-fiction quotient with *Lost in Space*; NBC itself, liking the concept but not the first pilot, Roddenberry's 'The Cage', commissioned a second, written by Samuel Peeples, 'Where No Man Has Gone Before'. In contrast to all the staffs of the *Trek* series that followed, *Star Trek*'s creative team had no idea that some viewers would rewatch each episode many times with hermeneutical zeal, first in reruns and then on video. When Captain Kirk's middle initial changed from R to T, when

The *Enterprise*
NCC-1701

the natives of Mr Spock's planet went from being referred to as Vulcanians to being referred to as Vulcans, when the force fields protecting the ship went back and forth between being deflector screens and deflector shields, no one could have been concerned at the inconsistencies. They were too busy trying to shoot episodes in six days with budgets inadequate to the production of space-based, futuristic science fiction, and to pull in viewers to watch episodes *once* in sufficient numbers to avoid cancellation.

It is also necessary to consider whether even within this one series an identical set of creative goals remained constant throughout. Roddenberry kept his eye on the general direction the show would take over the first two seasons, but, as Joel Engel points out, his influence came through his rewriting of others' scripts rather than taking an idea through story development and on to a finished teleplay.[13] Of his ten script credits on *Star Trek* (and three on *TNG*), only two were as the sole credited writer: his first pilot 'The Cage', as adapted for the two-part episode 'The Menagerie', and the much-reworked 'The Omega Glory', which had originally been submitted as a possible second pilot script. I will delineate Roddenberry's preoccupations below, but, in general, he preferred that *Star Trek* showcase people under threat struggling to survive and to do the right thing, but often having to take actions they regretted.

After the first part of the first season, Roddenberry still rewrote and polished scripts but was no longer the head writer-producer. John D. F. Black, who took on that role, became unhappy with Roddenberry's constant tinkering and quickly left, but his successor, Gene L. Coon, presided over a year of the best episodes in the series, and received screen credit on more of them – twelve – than any other *Star Trek* writer. Coon 'put more emphasis on the humorous elements within the show, particularly focusing on the sarcastic interplay between McCoy and Spock'.[14] Coon was also much more of a pacifist than Roddenberry and wrote several episodes in which the crew of the *Enterprise* achieved a *modus vivendi* with apparently hostile and implacable alien foes.

Another voice which contributed substantially to the *Star Trek* universe belonged to Dorothy 'D. C.' Fontana, who had teleplay credits for six episodes. She did much to flesh out the psychological contours of Spock and McCoy in episodes like 'This Side of Paradise', 'Friday's Child', 'Journey to Babel' and 'The Enterprise Incident', in all of these using their interactions with women to reveal both hidden strengths and hidden vulnerabilities. A Fontana speciality is the emotionally charged confrontation between two people who love each other when one must of necessity take an action harmful to the other.

When *Star Trek* gained a third season only to be given a reduced budget and a Friday 10pm time slot that conflicted with its young audience's dating behaviour, both Roddenberry and Fontana ceased active participation in the writing process. Coon had already departed some months before. Although their names appear on some third season episodes, the result of stories or draft teleplays being dusted off and produced, none of them was guiding the direction of the series. That duty fell to Fred Freiberger. He adhered to the broad thematic parameters established in the first two seasons, but episodes generally lacked the energy and narrative drive of the Roddenberry and Coon days. Freiberger did increase the number of topical and issue-oriented episodes and those dealing with the crew's romantic involvements. Nevertheless, none of these shifts in emphasis radically altered the

programme's template, and the distinction that most viewers recognise
in season three is a precipitous decline in overall quality.

The Kirk–Spock–McCoy Dynamic

The distinctiveness of *Star Trek*, the source of its massive pop-cultural
resonance, begins with its characters. The heterogeneity of the *Star Trek*
series regulars resides less in their racial and ethnic differences than in
pronounced demarcations in temperament and ideology, and these are
the true markers of diversity on the original series. None of the
characters is particularly complex and multilayered as a personality.
They are vivid and larger than life, however, and easily became iconic. A
few words or a tagline could summon up the essential and basically
static nature of each of them: 'Hailing frequencies open', 'Fascinating',

McCoy, Kirk and Spock

'He's dead, Jim', 'It was inwented by a Russian', 'Course plotted and laid in', the apocryphal 'Beam me up, Scotty'. The energy that truly propelled the *Enterprise* came not from the reactions of matter and anti-matter but from the power generated when these entirely predictable archetypes rubbed up against each other. In neither of the two pilots was the core ensemble complete, and it was wise of NBC to choose for the premiere episode the sixth one shot, 'The Man Trap', not because it was of exceptionally high quality but because the essential characteristics of the Kirk, Spock and McCoy trio in particular had gelled by that point, and the sparks provided by their differences were already flying.

It's customary to arrange this triumvirate along a continuum of logic and emotions, Spock at one end, McCoy at the other, with Kirk representing an optimal balance. In 'The Man Trap', Spock shows himself unable to comprehend Uhura's 'illogical' romantic longings to stroll in the moonlight and is then chastised by her for his stoic response to news that one of the landing party has died, since it might be the captain, 'the closest thing you have to a friend'. On the other hand, Kirk berates McCoy for becoming distracted by the presence of his lost love: 'You could learn something from Mr Spock, Doctor. Stop thinking with your glands.'

Yet there is more to this dynamic than positions on a scale of emotionality. For one thing, Kirk is himself highly emotional and impulsive, these traits emphasised by William Shatner's oft-parodied, melodramatic line readings. Struggling to find a balance between passion and intellect is indeed a major theme of the series, but it is a struggle seen in all three of the leading characters and in nearly every other life form the ship encounters. A more productive way to differentiate between Kirk, Spock and McCoy is to look at their approaches to problem-solving.

McCoy may be highly emotional, but he rarely acts upon emotion. Emotions drive people to make foolish, spur-of-the moment decisions, and this is not what 'Bones' does. He is a cautious proponent of the status quo, invariably warning that a course of action is untried or too risky. His southern American roots and courtly behaviour, his scepticism about technology such as the transporter, his self-identification as 'just an old country doctor' mark him as conservative almost to the point of being a reactionary. He is also a very limited thinker for a scientist. His initial reaction to a daring proposal from the captain is invariably to pronounce it undoable – he shares this trait with Chief Engineer Scott – or to declare it outside his field of expertise: 'I'm a doctor, not a mechanic, bricklayer, etc.' When he does come up with miracle cures for various alien diseases, it's because Spock or Kirk provides him with the outside-the-box theory that leads to the discovery ('The Deadly Years', 'Operation: Annihilate!'). He is quick to pronounce that a corpse is indeed a corpse; no heroic measures – not even CPR – are tried to reverse what may only be clinical death: thus the paradox of a healer whose tagline became 'He's dead, Jim.'

If (or because) relatively helpless in the face of death, McCoy becomes the leading advocate for preserving the living. His is the consistent 'dove' position in episodes where 'we make war to prevent war' scenarios are advanced ('Balance of Terror', 'A Private Little War'). McCoy is a humanist in the best sense, but also in the worst. His conservatism extends to befuddlement with things alien, and his constant sparring with Spock, based in their very different personalities and worldviews, is much too quick to descend into essentialist arguments based on Spock's different physiology, especially his green blood and tapered ears. These often skate very close to outright bigotry. Is it so different that he calls the Vulcan 'You pointed-eared hobgoblin' ('Bread and Circuses') than if he called Sulu 'You slanted-eyed samurai'?

Spock is above name-calling but does express a reciprocal disdain for humans, based not on their physical differences from Vulcans but upon their inability to filter out the emotional and the irrational and to proceed upon empirical reasoning only. Spock makes decisions based on the analysis of data – the name fittingly given to the android who performed his character function in *TNG*. Prone to calculating times and distances down to the second decimal place and quoting equally precise odds on the likelihood of various events taking place, Spock is the perfect empiricist, even if the scripts tweak him as too anally retentive. Unlike McCoy, Spock is eager to encounter the new and strange and will take fairly big risks if it will help him add to the database he uses for decision-making. Spock is also much more able to see all sides of a question and less likely to be swayed by mere ideology. He articulates persuasive rationales for Kirk not to disregard the Prime Directive and destroy the computers that provide peaceful, if soulless, societies in 'The Return of the Archons' and 'The Apple'. Yet he is perfectly willing to destroy an adversary if he sees no logical way to prevent it from threatening others. He recommends that the mutated Gary Mitchell (Gary Lockwood) be killed, long before Kirk can work himself up to the decision to execute the creature that has replaced the man who was once his friend. It is he who in 'The City on the Edge of Forever' convinces Kirk that 'Edith Keeler [Joan Collins] must die' in order to restore the past to its previous shape. He is also the most hawkish on stopping the Romulan ship in 'Balance of Terror', reasoning that its escape must inevitably signal Federation weakness and result in a massive Romulan invasion. As the series progressed and Spock became a counter-culture icon, his advocacy of deadly expediency waned and his non-violent temperament took precedence. Leonard Nimoy introduced the Vulcan neck pinch so that Spock, a vegetarian, would not engage in fistfights. Since so much violence is the result of overheated passions, passions which Vulcan logic holds in check, this makes perfect sense. Unlike humans, Vulcans don't 'kill without reason'. But as Spock admits in 'Journey to Babel', with his father Sarek (Mark Lenard) suspected of murder, when they do have a reason, Vulcans will kill efficiently.

27

However, Spock's database can never suffice for explicating every strange, new phenomenon the *Enterprise* encounters, at least not in crisis situations where there is no time to conduct a study. This is Spock's Achilles heel, the limitation that makes his efforts at solo command uniformly disastrous. Hoping respectively to deflect an asteroid ('The Paradise Syndrome') and retrieve Kirk from an alternate universe ('The Tholian Web') by calculating the physics of the situations, Spock finds his plans derailed by unexpected intrusions that render his mathematics inadequate. In 'The Galileo Seven', Spock is unable to get the stranded, off-course shuttlecraft into a stable orbit because he miscalculates the next moves of the planet's hostile natives, who fail to act upon rational principles. When death seems certain, he impulsively jettisons and ignites the remaining fuel supply in hopes of signalling their location to the *Enterprise*. Although Scotty believes that the action can have no more effect than sending up a flare, it does in fact bring about their rescue. In the logic of *Star Trek*, the capability to follow 'human' instincts to arrive at unorthodox solutions often marks the difference between success and failure.

Going by intuition, feeling his way, playing hunches and taking risks: these are the essence of Kirk's tactical thinking. The signature iconic game for *Star Trek* is three-dimensional chess and the logician Spock is its chief devotee. Yet Kirk routinely defeats him because of his intuitive strategies. Nevertheless, as illustrated in 'The Corbomite Maneuver', the game the captain is made for is poker. Or perhaps we should say that his best game is one he can make up as he goes along, demonstrated in the comic scene in 'A Piece of the Action' in which Kirk instructs his gangster captors on the rules of the imaginary 'fizzbin' by way of distraction. References to gambling, improvising, playing the odds permeate the series.

Kirk also comes upon many of his brilliant improvisations due to a casual external stimulus that enables him to cut the Gordian knot. Indeed, he is often the unlikely one to resolve scientific problems that have Spock and McCoy stymied. A prime instance occurs in 'Operation: Annihilate!'. A Denevan victim of the invasive, mind-controlling organisms that have infested all the inhabitants of that planet flies a ship into the sun, declaring himself free of the organisms before his craft burns up. Spock and McCoy consider every possible physical and chemical property of the sun and bombard a sample organism with them, to no effect. As they recite a list of these properties, Kirk notices a blinking indicator on a console, and has his epiphany: the sun is very, very bright. 'There's nothing lethal about light,' McCoy scoffs. Because both he and Spock have no records in their databases of organisms

Kirk sees the light

killed directly by shining bright lights on them, they dismiss a very obvious solution that Kirk immediately grasps.

That Kirk's salient characteristic is to go with his instincts reflects the deep-seated scepticism *Star Trek* expresses about expertise and empirical reasoning. Yet the portrayal of the captain does not gloss over the pitfalls of the intuitive approach and the limitations of James T. Kirk's particular psychology. First of all, his transcending of mere fact can become a dangerous disregarding of facts. 'Four hundred people; they'll die because I couldn't see a warning sign,' he berates himself in 'The Apple'. Kirk has to be skilled at saving the ship from danger because his impetuous command style often puts it in jeopardy. Lacking an empirical basis for many decisions puts undue emphasis on such a slender reed as human intuition. Kirk also is slow to perceive emotional distress in others. McCoy diagnoses that something is very 'off' with Spock as he enters *pon farr*, the Vulcan mating cycle, in 'Amok Time', but Kirk dismisses his concern at first by assigning the cause of aberrant behaviour to Spock being in 'one of his contemplative moods'. (If McCoy is too ready to give up hope of curing problems, Kirk is frequently too hesitant to recognise that problems exist.)

Relying on his own instincts has as its corollary a more generalised insensitivity to others' needs and opinions, a drift towards obsessiveness and self-doubt, and a tendency to lash out at his colleagues when he can't get a handle on things. Subordinates can be chastised for providing too little information or offering too many opinions. Kirk also in desperate situations elevates his gut feelings above adherence to the rules of the military organisation he serves, skirts the Prime Directive and insults Federation superiors like Nilz Baris (William Schallert) in 'The Trouble With Tribbles' or Commodore Stocker (Charles Drake) in 'The Deadly Years'. If Spock or Bones persists in questioning a course of action, Kirk can even sound downright Nixonian, especially given Shatner's narcissistic performance style. Murderous villains often hail Kirk as a kindred spirit. Needless to say, no one has written a manual on successful management techniques modelled on Kirk's example, as has been done with *TNG*'s Picard.[15]

For dramatic effect, however, the exhilaration of Kirk 'intuiting' himself out of difficulty is hard to match. Here is a *TV Guide* thirty-fifth anniversary tribute to a '*Trek*-tacular Moment' in 'The Deadly Years':

> After being cured of a bizarre case of premature aging that had turned him into a feeble old man, Kirk bounds onto the bridge in the midst of a Romulan attack and retakes control of the *Enterprise* from Commodore Stocker . . . the clueless greenhorn who'd had him relieved of command. . . . But there's a *real* leader in charge now, and it takes Kirk about a nanosecond to trick the Romulans into believing the ship is going to use a powerful corbomite device to self-destruct and that the explosion will destroy them, too. The bluff reveals the captain at his commanding best: cool, clever, daring, decisive and witty.[16]

For all his faults, then, *Star Trek* presents Kirk as an ego ideal for the audience. Because he does not possess any particular body of professional knowledge – he is not a scientist, doctor or engineer – he presents a wider space for audience identification. Anyone who has ever cleverly solved a problem or proved an overbearing superior deficient can imagine Kirk's brilliant improvisations as his or her own.

Through Kirk, *Star Trek* addresses the mainstream American television audience; he embodies many traits of the archetypal American hero.[17] Yet, situated within the Kirk–Spock–McCoy dynamic, the captain is not the only point of entry into the text. In the jocular sparring matches that became a trademark coda for the show, none of the three ever gets the other to admit defeat, and if Kirk's decisions invariably earn pragmatic validation, the opposing opinions of Spock or McCoy are never wholly invalidated. Through the central trio, a wide range of subject-identification becomes possible. One thinks of the typical cliques that form in high schools, their members rarely interacting. Kirk is the sports hero who is also president of the student council, Spock the brainy geek who runs the chess club and McCoy the regular guy with lots of friends who hangs out at the corner soda shop (or, now, the shopping centre). Probably more utopian than any of its social theory was *Star Trek*'s insistence that there was a community where all three types mattered and respected what each other could contribute.

Even as any of the three men at one time or the other offers to sacrifice his life for one or both of the others, there are moments in which they really don't like each other. This is especially true of Spock and McCoy. Smoothing over the antagonism between the doctor and the science officer is their mutual devotion to their captain. For its time, *Star Trek*'s fascination with the workings of male friendships and its openness in depicting raw manifestations of male emotional vulnerability were hardly the norm. It is, moreover, the scaffolding that supported even the weakest of its genre plots. 'The Immunity Syndrome', for example, is a dramatic and moving hour despite the fact that it is a 'creature feature' concerning the *Enterprise*'s being swallowed by a giant, energy-consuming space amoeba that is about to reproduce and suck all life out of the galaxy. At its core the episode is a meditation on how humanoids deal with the possibility of extinction. As it continues, the usual hostilities that inevitably break out between Spock and McCoy get mapped onto a type of sibling rivalry, as each makes a case for being allowed to undertake the very likely suicidal mission of piloting a shuttlecraft into the organism's nucleus. Kirk has to make the Solomonic choice. 'Dr McCoy has the medical and biological knowledge. Mr Spock is better suited physically and emotionally to stand the stress,' he records in his log. 'Both are right, both are capable and which of my friends do I condemn to death?' He chooses Spock, who claims that he cannot understand McCoy's competitiveness and emotional distress over what was a logical, impersonal decision. Yet Spock clearly feels gratified that the captain, who often joins Bones in teasing him about perceived lapses into human emotionalism, realises the value of its absence when the chips are down. Furthermore, Vulcan or no, he quite enjoys rubbing it in.

32

The climax of 'The Immunity Syndrome' demonstrates the multiple registers of emotion nearly always operating among Kirk, Spock and McCoy. As the *Enterprise* is fleeing the imminent explosion that should destroy the organism, the crew spot Spock's powerless shuttle and let him know that they will tow him out, despite risks that he advises them are too high to take. 'Shut up, Spock, we're rescuing you,' shouts McCoy. Spock, of course, replies sarcastically, 'Why thank you, *Captain* McCoy.' As they continue to wrangle over Spock's scientific findings, Kirk puts his foot down, telling the doctor with both relief and exasperation, 'Later, Bones, later.'

And there would always be a later. Science fiction often works to confound expectations, to disorient, to invalidate ingrained ideas about sentient behaviour and encrusted ideologies. The later *Trek* shows would all do so to a far greater extent than *Star Trek*. Its characters rather offer a direct access to a variety of archetypal emotional states and reward the regular viewer with the pleasures of the predictable.

Looking Ahead, with Dread

The stories that *Star Trek* tells and retells stem from its overarching
concern about the many possible futures that might await the human
species. And most of them are not at all utopian, despite the many
statements about *Trek*'s optimism that characterise the fan discourse
that Gene Roddenberry adopted and promulgated as the show reached
cult status in the 1970s. Wagner and Lundeen give a succinct statement
of the party line as espoused by the 'Great Bird of the Galaxy' and those
who fed and fed on his mythologising of himself:

> Foremost among the tenets of Roddenberry's vision is humanism – a
> compassion for our species and a faith in its ultimate wisdom and capacity
> for self-reliance. Bolstering this central premise are an optimistic view of
> the human future; an emphasis on the imperatives of freedom, growth and
> change; a tolerance of diversity; a central role for the emotions of
> friendship and loyalty; an opposition to prejudice or tradition-for-its-own-
> sake; and a visceral rejection of organized religion and divine authority.[18]

They also assert that this 'unifying, hopeful vision' has made '*Trek* so
beloved and so durable'. I wouldn't disagree with their conclusion, but
the premise upon which it is based derives from a hopeful and wilful
misreading of the collective text that is the original *Star Trek*. To be sure,
imagining that Earth's various nations would band together to form a
space fleet, after averting a nuclear holocaust and solving many social
problems, did look wildly utopian from the vantage point of the late
1960s. Yet once humans move out into space, the same problems
reappear. Instead of nations competing with each other on one planet,
Earth becomes one planet with other planetary allies and adversaries
trying to avert the same sorts of cataclysmic conflicts on a galactic scale.
Indeed, many commentators have seen the relations between the
Federation, the Klingons and the Romulans as a replica of Cold War
tensions between the USA, the Soviet Union and China.[19] Those of
European, Asian and African descent might celebrate their unity in

33

diversity aboard the ship, but inter-species prejudice is alive and well and not the sole purview of non-human aliens.

In 'Balance of Terror' Kirk is stern in reprimanding Lt Stiles (Paul Comi) for voicing his suspicions of Spock being a Romulan spy: 'Leave any bigotry in your quarters. There's no room for it on the bridge.' Notice that Kirk does not dismiss the possibility of one of his officers being a bigot. He merely states that such prejudice has no place in the functioning of the *Enterprise* crew. That humans are still quite capable of being goaded into expressions of racial hatred is made clear repeatedly in regard to Spock. Whenever some undue influence is stressing out the crew, as in 'Day of the Dove', they are likely to respond to him with anti-Vulcan slurs. For McCoy this is a regular occurrence, which Spock only challenges when he is, in turn, affected by the trip through the Atavachron in 'All our Yesterdays'. As McCoy starts another 'You pointed-eared Vulcan' rant Spock lays hands on him and replies, 'I don't like that. I don't think I ever did, and now I'm sure.' Even when the bigotry is feigned, as Kirk does to rouse Spock to anger in 'This Side of Paradise', one can't help but notice the nasty specificity of the slurs that come all too easily to Kirk's tongue:

> All right you mutinous, disloyal, computerised half-breed. We'll see about you taking over my ship . . . Does [that girl] know what she's getting, Spock, a carcass full of memory banks who should be squatting on a mushroom instead of passing himself off as a man? You belong in a circus, Spock, not a starship – right next to the dog-faced boy.

Spock's disdain for human behaviour doesn't leave him exempt from charges of prejudice either, although his expressions of it are generally more subtle than those directed at him.

If the *Enterprise* crew is not immune from twentieth-century human failings, Starfleet's record contains an equal amount of human failure. Many times the *Enterprise* returns to the site where a former Earth vessel has been lost, its crew leaving behind some deleterious effects on other planets that the *Enterprise* crew has to remedy. By the time the series is over, it is apparent that Kirk and his colleagues represent a charmed exceptionalism by surviving the hazards of space that have claimed so many other Starfleet lives. Yet even their survival often has a heavy cost, and triumph is consistently tinged with regret. The last words spoken in the final episode were 'If only . . .', and although that particular episode, 'Turnabout Intruder', fraught with misogyny, does not rank as one of the series' shining hours, its concluding sentiment is quite appropriate.

Beginning with the premise that humankind will survive its destructive conflicts to encounter hostile sentient life forms from other solar systems and other galaxies, *Star Trek* therefore asks, 'Now what?' The answers are rarely untroubled. For instance, the foundational statement about humans is that they must struggle against obstacles so as to grow and change, or they will stagnate and die. Kirk has several arias that enunciate this principle:

> Our species can only survive if we have obstacles to overcome. You take away all obstacles. Without them to strengthen us, we will weaken and die. ('Metamorphosis')

35

> No wants, no needs. We weren't meant for that, none of us. Man stagnates if he has no ambition, no desire to be more than he is. . . . Maybe we don't belong in paradise, Bones. Maybe we're meant to fight our way through. Struggle, claw our way up, fighting every inch of the way. Maybe we can't stroll to the music of lutes; we must march to the sound of drums. ('This Side of Paradise')

If this is true, then the species will inevitably evolve and change. Yet, as the *Enterprise* roams the galaxy, the more highly evolved species it meets don't exactly provide attractive evolutionary end points. A number evolve themselves completely out of material existence, others reach a peak and then regress and stagnate, still others become incorporeal tyrants who require the unquestioning obedience of subjugated humanoids in order to survive.

That so many highly evolved beings develop into a pure form of consciousness while material bodies wither away is the second primal fear of *Star Trek*, and the converse of its first, that sapient beings will become content to sit mindlessly in perpetuity in some Arcadian paradise. For *Star Trek* cannot imagine being 'human' without being embodied. Sapience unincarnated is invariably represented as monstrous. Definitely on the 'body' side of the eternal mind/body duality, *Star Trek* nevertheless finds the demands of vulnerable, desiring flesh the surest obstacle to short-term species survival and the strongest temptation to cast aside individual integrity. So, as I delineate the various answers to 'What next?' that the series ponders, I must first look at physical desire.

Girls in Space Be Wary

One project of recent popular writing about *Trek* has been the demythologising of Gene Roddenberry and his claim to sole authorship of the first series and of the *Trek* universe. Reports from collaborators detailing how Roddenberry appropriated their ideas and called them his own are legion, of a critical mass too great to attribute to mere sour grapes. From the scholarly perspective, no such testimony is necessary to assure that analysis of the televisual text is not tied to some perception of its author. Nevertheless, one aspect of Roddenberry's life looms so large in biographical accounts and dovetails so clearly with one of *Star Trek*'s obsessively reiterated tropes that it cannot be ignored: he was a compulsive womaniser and may well have been a sex addict. Solow recalls,

> It was tough to ignore his constantly straying eye whenever a woman was near. If it wore a skirt, or looked like it should be wearing a skirt, Roddenberry's radar locked on instantly. You had to feel he'd accepted the earthly role of Adam, playing to hundreds, maybe thousands of Eves. Young, old, large, small, beautiful, homely, it made no difference – as long as the Miss or Mrs or Madame conceivably might be available.[20]

Mudd's women

Unless she were playing a very small, purely functionary role, a woman on *Star Trek* is always conspicuously available. A featured guest actress is usually introduced through a gauzy close-up while the soundtrack plays the same syrupy melody, one that quickly became a shorthand for 'look, attractive female here'. The women's costumes are famously revealing, pushing the boundaries of broadcast standards at the time. As if projecting a defence against accusations of caddish philandering (as well as playing to male fantasies), the men of the *Enterprise* are rarely the pursuers. In a number of episodes ('Mudd's Women', 'A Private Little War', 'Elaan of Troyius') female seductiveness becomes almost irresistible because chemically induced, the science-fiction redaction of the Circe myth. Women often use their sexuality to enslave, exploit, or lure men to their doom, but Kirk more than reciprocates. With the exceptions of Edith Keeler in 'The City on the Edge of Forever' and Rayna (Louise Sorel) in 'Requiem for Methuselah', Kirk's current interest in a woman is prompted by his need to seduce her in order to save himself or his ship. Of those he actually loves, he facilitates the deaths of Edith and Rayna, and the parade of women he has loved and left behind leaves

37

little doubt that Kirk cannot make a commitment. As McCoy remarks to one of the captain's former lovers, Areel Shaw (Joan Marshall), in 'Court Martial': 'All of my old friends look like doctors, all of his look like you.'

Yet, there is more going on here than the creation of a James Bond ethos in the Swinging 60s or the portrayal of a crew stuck in the latency stage of development.[21] In the first part of the show's first season, during which Roddenberry rewrote all the episodes, a sense of sexual attraction as a powerful and tragic force predominates over the occasional leering remarks. Desire is a paradox: something one can barely survive without succumbing to and yet a path to ruin if one does succumb. It's there in McCoy's and Dr Crater's (Alfred Ryder) inability to destroy the salt vampire when it takes the form of the Nancy (Jeanne Bal) they both loved; in Charlie Evans' (Robert Walker Jr) longing for Janice Rand (Grace Lee Whitney), which almost leads him to destroy her; in the real connection that arises amid the mutual manipulations of Lenore Karidian (Barbara Anderson) by Kirk and Kirk by Lenore. Women's pain at abandonment or betrayal by men they long for features strongly during the first season as well, from Miri's (Kim Darby) schoolgirl crush to Vina's (Susan Oliver) need for Christopher Pike's (Jeffrey Hunter) affections. Dorothy Fontana's 'This Side of Paradise' is one of the most poignant takes on this theme.

Desire for any particular partner rarely survives its consummation. Love is celebrated in the breach but trivialised in the observance. As Spock, in 'Amok Time', observes to his rival Stonn (Lawrence Montaigne) upon surrendering his promised bride to him, 'After a time you may find that having is not so pleasing a thing after all as wanting. It is not logical, but it is often true.' *Star Trek* does not attribute these commitment issues to mere randyness or buyer's regret, of course. For Kirk, a nobler and more powerful prior commitment exists, one which it was assumed the male viewer, at least, would find far more sacred than marriage vows made to a mere female. His id laid bare in 'The Naked Time', Kirk laments, 'This vessel, I give, she takes; she won't permit me my life. Now I know why they call it she.' Despite articulating an urge to give up command so that he can walk on a beach with a beautiful flesh and blood woman, it is to the *Enterprise* that he whispers, 'Never lose you, never.'

When Spock chooses duty over love, on the other hand, the motivation is less a commitment to the ship and its mission than it is personal loyalty to Kirk. He states the equation with logical precision in 'Amok Time': 'Oh, yes, the girl. It must have been the combat. When I thought I'd killed the captain, I lost all interest in T'Pring [Arlene Martel].' If this episode is particularly frank about how duty and loyalty trump desire, it is also the series' most overt consideration of male sexuality as a compulsive, annihilating force. The Vulcan *pon farr* propels the male into a period of sexual 'heat' so intense that he must either 'take a wife or die'. 'Amok Time' also acknowledges through the metaphorical biology of Vulcans the discomfort a man may feel if his urges overcome his reason: 'It strips our minds from us and brings a madness which rips away our veneer of civilisation.'

The women who serve aboard the *Enterprise* often face the same conflict between love and loyalty, with the difference being that love is the stronger lure. Dr Elizabeth Dehner (Sally Kellerman), Lt Marla McGivers (Madlyn Rhue) and Lt Carolyn Palamas (Leslie Parrish) initially side with Gary Mitchell, Khan (Ricardo Montalban) and Apollo (Michael Forest) even though these men to whom they are

39

Apollo and
Lt Carolyn Palamas

attracted pose a threat to the *Enterprise*. None goes so far as to permit their lovers to destroy the ship and crew, however. Thus, service in Starfleet is depicted for both sexes as a duty that must transcend a pervasive and strong sexual desire. Nevertheless, the intense pain that the mutual exclusivity of duty and desire exacts informs the series in a profound way that the skimpy female costumes and long line of Kirk's ex-girlfriends can obscure. It is also far in excess of that demanded by the conventions of television action-adventure shows at the time, in which the male protagonists remained single and unattached, any deep romantic involvement destined to end badly.

Brain and Brain!

While the renunciation of desire becomes a positive trait when viewed in terms of duty to a higher calling and mapped upon typical male paradigms of striving and sacrifice beyond the domestic sphere, it accompanies in *Star Trek* a corollary that provokes alarm rather than admiration. The utopian pronouncements that valorise progress and exploration, that make traversing the final frontier a metaphor for the human species' evolutionary drive, are always shadowed here by the fear that the evolutionary end point mandates not just a denial but a withering away of physical passions and sexual potency. Many of the threats to the crew from non-humanoid aliens involve a sort of vampirism, a draining of crucial elements from the body. The shape-shifter of 'The Man Trap' sucks out all the body's salts. The deadly cloud in 'Obsession' drains red corpuscles. The Kelvans of 'By Any Other Name' have a device that reduces humans to friable blocks that look like (and probably are) styrofoam. These are times in which *Star Trek* comes close to articulating a paranoid subtext about an 'intergalactic alien conspiracy to sap and impurify all of our precious bodily fluids', to paraphrase *Dr Strangelove*'s (1964) Col. Jack D. Ripper.

NBC's stated reason for rejecting 'The Cage' and asking for a second *Star Trek* pilot was that the script was 'too cerebral', and some reviewers of the *Star Trek* premiere echoed that concern. There is a profound irony here, for the explicit message of 'The Cage', and of *Star Trek* generally, is that sentient beings over-develop their intellectual capabilities at their peril. Within humans the danger is usually seen not so much as a mind/body dualism but as the conflict between reason and emotion, head and heart. It is the central focus of 'The Enemy Within'. Here a transporter accident doubles Kirk's body but splits his consciousness. One avatar retains the captain's moral sense and his rationality, yet he is weak and indecisive. The other is little more than 'a thoughtless brutal animal', driven by lust and crippled by fear, yet within him resides all that makes Kirk the superior commander he is. 'And what is it that makes one man an exceptional leader?' Spock observes. 'We see here indications that it is his negative side which makes him strong, that his evil side, if you will, properly controlled and disciplined is vital to his strength.' Only by literally embracing his irrational half can Kirk function fully.

Despite the association of the animalistic Kirk with a moral position – his 'evil side' – *Star Trek* has an asymmetrical approach when it comes to one or other of the two gaining ascendancy. While some episodes show the pitfalls of overwhelming passions, far more dwell on the dangers that follow when reason goes unchecked by emotion, when cranial capacity increases while physical strength wanes, or when consciousness detaches itself entirely from corporeality. Viewers rarely visit a planet where the inhabitants pursue physical perfection and sensual excess while intellect withers, except in tandem with some controlling, non-human intelligence that needs to turn humans into Eloi for its own ends. Yet countless times some 'big brain' proves a deadly adversary for the crew of the *Enterprise*.

Just as humans evolved from 'lower' and furrier mammalian species, much science fiction postulates that further evolution would culminate in oversized crania and hairless bodies. The Talosians of 'The Cage'/'The Menagerie' fit this bill perfectly. They have large, bald heads and slight, androgynous physiques. After a planetary catastrophe, they

41

The big-brained Talosians

become expert telepaths and are able to create convincing illusions based on the memories and desires of other sentient creatures. Unfortunately, the power is 'a trap': 'When dreams become more important than reality you give up travel, building, creating. You even forget how to repair the machines left by your ancestors,' their captive Vina explains. 'You just sit living and reliving other lives left in the thought record.' Like the obsessive fan of the show 'The Cage' would launch, the Talosians would be unable to 'get a life', and without generations of human slaves to rebuild their world for them, they are doomed to slow extinction. So incapacitating and potentially contagious is this power of illusion that Starfleet prohibits any further contact with Talos IV and imposes its only death penalty on anyone who violates this regulation. 'The Cage' sets out one of several paradigms for the over-balance of mental power in *Star Trek*. This is the case of species whose minds evolve to outstrip their physical capabilities, but which remain in corporeal form. Such creatures usually find themselves in need of humanoid guinea pigs or slaves to complete their existence. Often more desperate than depraved, they nevertheless think nothing of causing suffering to their captives in pursuit of their own goals.

Other species evolve beyond corporeal form altogether to become pure mental energy. These are less likely to interfere in humanoid affairs than to disdain them altogether, but any accidental contact shows them in a less than flattering light. In 'The Squire of Gothos' Trelane's parents chide him for mistreating his human 'pets', but the term is telling, and Trelane (William Campbell) amply demonstrates that the immature members of this incorporeal species are capable of great cruelty. One might also note that aliens who respectively crave the emotions of fear and anger in order to survive in 'Wolf in the Fold' and 'Day of the Dove' are energy beings as well. It is almost as if, without a physical form to generate strong emotions, they feel incomplete and must extract them from humanoid victims.

Unlike such creatures, the Organians in 'Errand of Mercy' occupy the moral high ground, but Kirk finds their humanoid manifestations craven and cowardly. Both he and the Klingon Kor (John Colicos) consider them sheep, when a ram or wolves are called for. The Thasians of 'Charlie X' are likewise benevolent in intention, but their very incorporeality is incompatible with the instincts and desires of the flesh. 'Don't let them take me. I can't even touch them,' Charlie pleads.

If these ominous de-incarnations threaten from far along the evolutionary path that human progress may reach in the coming millennia, there is also a clear and present danger to the crew of the *Enterprise* in their own day: the possibility that humankind will allow itself to be subjugated to the rule of the biggest of big brains, the inorganic super-computer. Dangerous computers, robots or androids turn up in twelve of the series' seventy-nine episodes. Their root deficiencies resemble those ascribed to Vulcan logic, and frequent comparisons of Spock to computers occur throughout the series. Likewise, cybernetic entities contemptuous of organic mental insufficiency usually consider Spock a cut above his human colleagues. Even Spock, however, acknowledges that 'computers make excellent

Kor and Kirk can't understand the Organians

and efficient servants, but I have no wish to serve under them' ('The Ultimate Computer'). When allowed to go unsupervised, often because they have 'outlived' their organic creators, computers take everything to the ultimate logical conclusions – which inevitably involves the AI deciding that it is far superior to humanoids and should either enslave them for what it concludes to be their own good ('I, Mudd', 'The Apple', 'The Return of the Archons') or destroy them if they threaten the survival of the superior machine ('The Changeling', 'The Ultimate Computer').

Computers arrive at this dangerous position for two reasons. First, they are capable neither of adapting their programming to changed circumstances nor of deviating from its rigid and narrow focus. Lacking compassion or intuition and clinging to fatally literal interpretations, they transform initially benevolent programming to serve and protect organics into its opposite. This is why Kirk can often paralyse them into inaction or self-destruction by pointing out that the means for taking care of organic charges has become incompatible with the end of their ultimate well-being. The second flaw is found in the inability of the cybernetic mind to discern errors within initial premises. Damage the Nomad probe suffered in space led it to mistake the name of James T. Kirk for that of Jackson Roykirk, its creator. When Kirk lures the machine into asserting first its own perfection and then its conviction that he is its creator, his triumphant 'You're wrong!' convicts the machine of 'error' and incapacitates it.

By *Star Trek* logic, what redeems Spock from his uncomfortable resemblance to such machines is his submerged human half. Yet the series disavows such a possibility for AIs; there is no utopian, Donna Haraway view of cyborg identity here. Dr Richard Daystrom (William Marshall) achieves a breakthrough in 'multitronic' computing by impressing his own human engrams on the circuits of the M-5 unit. Unfortunately, the computer has absorbed its designer's near paranoid resentment of those colleagues who have condescended to the boy wonder who won the Nobel and Zee-Magnees prizes in his early twenties but has worked fruitlessly for the next twenty years trying to top himself. As Spock explains, the M-5 is 'a human mind amplified by the instantaneous relays possible in a computer'. If that mind is in the grip of strong emotions, they will be blown so out of proportion that the machine goes insane. Thus, when the android Rayna apparently achieves a truly human consciousness, the amplified, conflicting emotions outrun the capabilities of her circuitry, and she ceases to function.

Star Trek locates the deficiencies of mental energy beings or brains with inorganic bodies in what they both lack: humanoid flesh. The essential humanism of *Star Trek* has less to do with the secular, human-centred articulation of values that would dominate *TNG* than with the contention that consciousness residing anywhere but in an organic life form is, for lack of a better word, perverse. Other episodes thus work to inculcate the desirability of incarnation, despite simultaneously acknowledging all the sins that flesh is heir to. While

45

once-humanoid species who have evolved beyond their physical bodies may not regret the process, even if the *Enterprise* crew finds them less than satisfactory company, several alien species who have radically different physiologies but take on human form to function within human environments soon find themselves completely overcome by the sensuality that comes with the incarnation. This fate befalls members of an advance team of Kelvans, invading aliens from the Andromeda galaxy, in 'By Any Other Name'. Kirk and his senior officers defeat them but simultaneously win them over by provoking lust, anger, gluttony, jealousy – and emptying the entire contents of Scotty's liquor cabinet. *Star Trek* prefers the potentially destructive passions that flesh authorises to the psychic castration that results when big brains or other powerful aliens create paternalistic paradises for populations in exchange for a life free from strife and struggle. 'The Return of the Archons' delineates this theme most fully, especially as it reveals what the body means to a machine intelligence. The *Enterprise* discovers a world where the inhabitants' minds are controlled by a super-computer that houses the knowledge, but not the 'wisdom', of a long-dead leader, Landru (Charles Macaulay). The civilisation was once highly advanced but riven by violence, and he led them back to a simpler time. Any individual who cannot be absorbed into 'the body', as Landru conceptualises the society, must be destroyed as if he or she were an attacking infection. The Landru computer allows for periodic bacchanals during a prescribed 'Red Hour', but when it ends, the citizens go back to what Spock calls 'mindlessness, vacant contentment', wishing each other peace and tranquility. To Kirk this is merely 'the peace of the factory, the tranquility of the machine'. Landru, of course, sees the situation quite differently: 'A world without hate, without fear without conflict: no war, no disease, no crime – none of the ancient evils. … Your individuality will merge into the unity of good and in your submergence into the common being of the body you'll find contentment, fulfilment, you will experience the absolute good.' It unfortunately fails to see that by killing any who resist being absorbed into the body politic, it is engaging in just those ancient evils.

46

Landru

In their overview of the cluster of episodes about such 'hellish heavens', Wagner and Lundeen conclude, 'Paradise is a form of cowardice, by which we give up our freedom of thought and choice, our individuality and our capacity for passion – all in exchange for safety, security and ease.'[22] This is indeed the assertion the episodes make, but it is always a loaded one. What if the inhabitants of Beta III had chosen to live peacefully and to trade progress and ambition for peace and contentment, without coercion? Contemporary fears of communist collectivism or blissed-out youth drug cultures underlie the stacking of the decks (although Spock always points out the benefits of happy stagnation). The overriding fear, as it is in all the cautionary tales of letting head prevail over heart (or Philia over Eros, as Wagner and Lundeen put it), is of emasculation. A few of Landru's subjects are immune to the effects of the mind control, and they have formed a resistance movement, inspired by the *Archon* crew whom Landru could not subdue. They still fear their leader, however, and hope that Kirk and his companions will free them. He is not impressed. 'Snap out of it. Start acting like men,' he tells them. 'Freedom is never a gift. It has to be earned.' When he has destroyed Landru, he contemptuously addresses the leader of the resistance, 'Well, Marplon [Torin Thatcher], you're on your own. I hope you're up to it.' In all the episodes that portray regressive societies controlled by a big brain there is some sort of deviation from 'normal' sexuality.

Putting things right invariably demands the reinstitution of male prerogatives and the integration of passion and individual will. Interestingly, one of the necessary passions is anger. Sociologist Lindstrom (Christopher Held) reports that after the destruction of Landru, conditions on the planet 'couldn't be better'. He continues, 'Already this morning we've had half a dozen domestic quarrels and two genuine knock-down drag-outs. It may not be Paradise – but it's certainly human.' Anger and hatred are also the tools used respectively by Kirk and Captain Pike to free humans from control of the spores on Omicron Ceti III and to prevent the Talosians from reading human thoughts. Wagner and Lundeen note, 'In a broad sense, anger and conflict are portrayed as a humanizing force in these narratives precisely because a one-sided pursuit of harmony and peace has become the vehicle of dehumanization.'[23] This begs the question of why such a binary should be present in *Star Trek*. The disturbing answer is that 'acting like men' correlates uncomfortably with acting violently.

By contrast, those organic beings who abhor violence and eschew anger are inevitably portrayed either by older male actors as asexual ('Errand of Mercy') or by women playing androgynous males ('Arena', 'The Menagerie'). When Kirk, in 'The Apple', strikes Vaal's humanoid liaison Akuta (Keith Andes), he weeps. Significantly, the primary mode of conflict that breaks out on Beta III is the domestic disturbance. *Star Trek* paradises and *Star Trek* disembodiment negate the necessity for stereotypically male attributes such as exploration, competitiveness, or bread-winning. Elias Sandoval (Frank Overton) in 'This Side of Paradise' awakens from the spores to say, 'We've done nothing here, no accomplishments, no progress, three years wasted.' Leila Kalomi (Jill Ireland), on the other hand, is devastated by the loss of contentment and protests any assertion that it was done for her good. The domestic tranquility of paradise is feminising, and it takes manly eruptions of fistfights for its yoke to be overthrown. In contrast to traditional equations of masculinity with reason and femininity with emotion and the body, *Star Trek* celebrates the 'sensate body' of the male and links logic to emasculation, violent passion to virility and virility to human identity. This opens up a paradox at the heart of the series, since it purports to describe a future in which humankind overcame its instinct for violence.

We're Not Going to Kill ... Today

Navigating this paradox became the special purview of Gene L. Coon. In a cluster of late first season episodes – 'Arena', 'A Taste of Armageddon', 'The Devil in the Dark' and 'Errand of Mercy' – he creates situations in which self-preservation seems to demand that humanoids fight and kill, and yet they find the means not to do so. In 'Arena', a previously unknown alien race, the Gorn, wipe out a Federation colony on Cestus 3. Kirk goes off in hot pursuit with the goal of destroying their vessel, even though Spock cautions that they have not yet heard the Gorns' side of the story. They wander into territory controlled by the highly advanced Metrons, who seize Kirk and the Gorn captain and put them on an uninhabited planet that contains sufficient raw materials for each to fashion weapons deadly to the other. As the battle progresses, Kirk learns that the Gorn claim the space in which Cestus 3 is located and regard the Federation as an invading force. When Kirk constructs a primitive cannon that disables the Gorn, he refuses to kill him. At that point a Metron reveals itself and remarks:

49

> By sparing your helpless enemy, who surely would have destroyed you, you demonstrated the advanced trait of mercy, something we hardly expected. We feel there may be hope for your kind . . . Perhaps in several thousand years, your people and mine shall meet to reach an agreement. You are still half-savage, but there is hope. We will contact you when we are ready.

Kirk and Spock confront the Horta

50

In 'Devil' Kirk spares the 'monstrous' silicon-based Horta (Janos Prohaska) after it pleads/promises 'No Kill I'; the alien may have killed a number of human miners, but it did so only to protect its children. Here no more advanced race has to set the conditions of the test. Kirk passes it on his own. Conversely, in 'Errand of Mercy' Kirk desires a fight every bit as strongly as does the Klingon commander, and the Organians essentially have to take away both species' ability to wage war in order to halt the conflict.

Coon's definitive statement on how humanoids can arrive at peaceful coexistence rather than mutual annihilation comes in 'A Taste of Armageddon', in which Kirk takes on the Organians' role in regard to the Emenians, who have sustained a 500-year-long war with the neighbouring planet of Vendikar. The episode links *Star Trek*'s dovish leanings with its distrust of computer logic, because this war has only continued because it is totally computerised. It is as sanitised as the video-game conflicts that would emerge in the coming decades. No infrastructures crumble, and economies do not collapse from devoting resources to the manufacture and development of weapons and maintaining standing armies. There is a price in lives, but death comes cleanly and painlessly as those tagged as casualties by the computers surrender to disintegration stations. In short, war is disembodied: no pain, no screams, no blood, no mutilations.

By *Star Trek*'s logic the anger and violence that inhere in humanoid bodies – and which the series valorises to a surprising extent – do start wars, but other bodily sensations, those that feel suffering, act as a counterbalance, allowing reason to step in and defeat war. Thus, when Anan7 (David Opatoshu), the Emenian leader, asserts that killing is inherent in the species, Kirk responds:

> All right, it's instinctive but the instinct can be fought. We're human beings with the blood of a million savage years on our hands. But we can stop it. We can admit that we're killers but were not going to kill today. That's all it takes – knowing that we're not going to kill . . . today.

51

While the *Trek* universe would offer a number of divergent paths to the overcoming of violence, such as the Vulcan discipline of logic and the evolution of species into incorporeality and beyond passion, *Star Trek* would rather that the potentially murderous 'enemy within' be governed but never repressed or extirpated.

Coon's scripts posit situations in which choosing not to kill saves lives and does not leave either side vulnerable. Roddenberry, on the other hand, asserts that killing is regrettable but sometimes necessary. In several episodes for which he receives sole or partial writing credit – 'A Private Little War', 'The Omega Glory', 'The Savage Curtain' – he shows Kirk pushed into a fight or reluctantly backing one side of a conflict on a more primitive world. 'A Private Little War' ponders whether force can ever be used without corrupting those who use it. An obvious allegory of the Vietnam conflict, the original script by Don Ingalls was firmly dovish[24] and McCoy voices many of his arguments. By the time Roddenberry had rewritten it,

however, the episode advocated the US involvement in
Vietnam explicitly:

> Bones, do you remember the twentieth-century brush wars on the Asian
> continent, two giant powers involved, much like the Klingons and
> ourselves? Neither side felt that they could pull out. . . . What would you
> have suggested, that one side arm its friends with an overpowering weapon?
> Mankind would never have lived to travel space if they had. No, the only
> solution is what happened back then – balance of power . . . War isn't a
> good life, but it's life.

Roddenberry had articulated the belief that pacifism is
ineffective as a strategy for opposing evil in the pilot he wrote in 1963
for his proposed World War II series set in the Pacific, *APO 923*. US
soldiers attempt to convince some villagers to aid them in fighting the
Japanese. The village elder demurs, in words that could have come from
a Coon script: 'The greatest courage is not to kill – even in the face of
death.' The American captain argues that 'your way is maybe more
violent than ours . . . Just by sitting still and letting it happen you can
hurt more people than the rest of us who fight back.'[25] This is also the
message behind the most wrenching decision Kirk makes in all of *Star
Trek*, to let Edith Keeler die because the pacifist movement she would
have founded would have kept America out of the war until it was too
late to defeat Hitler. 'She was right, peace was the way,' Kirk muses, to
be reminded by Spock that 'she *was* right, but at the wrong time'.

Even Roddenberry turns non-combatant when conflicts go
beyond conventional weaponry, however. Cold War fears of nuclear
annihilation are never far from the surface in *Star Trek*, and prolonged
galactic war among alliances that possess powerful destructive weapons
is always forestalled. A firm stand against escalation in the creation of
weapons of mass destruction comes in 'The Doomsday Machine'. An
unstoppable planet killer, presumed to be 'a weapon built primarily as a
bluff', has nevertheless been launched in another galaxy; it now roams
the universe as a predator 'self-sustaining as long as there are planets for

it to feed on'. If *Star Trek* spends considerable time pondering the effect on humanoid species should they survive for eons and evolve beyond corporeal form, the spectre of such a weapon also puts its doubts about such evolution in the context of the much less fantastic scenario of species becoming extinct.

The Last of Their Kind

Nearly half the episodes of *Star Trek* refer to mass annihilations of populations. The numbers of casualties may be relatively small, such as the research stations wiped out in 'The Naked Time', 'The Empath', or 'The Lights of Zetar'; they can be the hundreds of Starfleet crew members lost in 'The Immunity Syndrome', 'The Doomsday Machine', or 'The Omega Glory'. But frequently the losses are in the millions or billions from hostile attacks on colonies, planets or whole inhabited solar systems, as in 'Balance of Terror', 'The Changeling', or 'Operation: Annihilate!'. Cataclysms due either to humanoid error or natural phenomena sometimes do not completely wipe out the inhabitants of a planet or system but force a bizarre twist in the species' evolution. The genetic experimentation in 'Miri' kills all the adults but allows pre-pubescent children to age extremely slowly, although they are still doomed when they finally reach puberty. No doubt because the producers had a cave set handy – such a set will be a staple of all *Trek* series – we frequently find the survivors forced underground, where they become dependent on computers and androids and/or fall into such cultural dysfunctions as the addiction to illusion of the Talosians or the alienation between the sexes and mental atrophy of both in 'Spock's Brain'. Sometimes only the computers survive the doomed organics, and they inevitably become dangerous to other humanoid species, as in 'What Are Little Girls Made Of?', 'I, Mudd' and 'That Which Survives'.

It is tempting to take all these episodes as cautionary tales, detailing mistakes humanity must not make if it is to survive. For the short term, this is certainly true. Yet many seem instead to stress the

53

The salt vampire

inevitability of the rise and fall of cultures. Particularly in episodes in which a single individual or very small group of individuals survive the end of a race, the message that holding on past one's time is dangerous gets considerable play. When a *Star Trek* species is reduced below a critical survival mass, it can only hold on through parasitism or exploitation of some kind. The creature on planet M-113 (Sharon Gimpel) is commonly referred to as 'the salt vampire' because it lives by sucking all the salts from human bodies after the supply of natural salt is exhausted on its planet. The Zetarans take over humanoid bodies so that their collective memory can survive.

Exemplary of imagined scenarios for the evolution of embodied sapient consciousness are the second season episodes 'Metamorphosis', written by Coon and giving his usual more utopian take on evolutionary parameters, and 'Return to Tomorrow', written by his successor as head writer, John Meredyth Lucas, and advancing the more prevalent minatory stance of the series as a whole. 'Metamorphosis' finds Kirk, Spock and McCoy hijacked by a cloud-like creature so that they can assuage the loneliness of the stranded human she has rejuvenated and rendered immortal, and to whom she serves as beneficent companion, providing for his needs. This is, however, not just any human but Zefram Cochrane (Glenn Corbett), the inventor of the warp drive and thus the enabler of the *Trek* universe. He is not only lonely but bored, and is eager to leave the planet and engage with a universe that offers many years of technological advances to savour. The Companion wants to keep him to herself. This sets up the familiar pattern in which a ruling computer or powerful alien wishes to keep humans in a pastoral setting, offer sustenance independent of effort and eliminate the fear of death, in exchange for their service and adoration.

Ordinarily, Kirk would persuade or coerce the controlling alien to self-immolate and release its subjects, but 'Metamorphosis' offers a compromise. The Companion is, in fact, in love with Cochrane, and it is a love she cannot fully consummate because of their radically different physiologies. Moreover, when Cochrane realises what's been going on, he is repulsed. Although Spock and McCoy are puzzled by Cochrane's 'parochial' reaction, *Star Trek* has little use for pure energy beings, and it's no surprise that even Coon can salvage the romance only by providing the Companion with human embodiment. When their shuttle was diverted, the *Enterprise* officers had been transporting the seriously ill Federation diplomat Nancy Hedford (Elinor Donahue) to a Starfleet medical facility. Hedford is an ill-tempered woman who has devoted herself to her career and never 'known love'. Such sexually unavailable women are even more anathema to the show's worldview than malevolent clouds of electricity, so the perfect solution is found when the Companion merges with Hedford, producing an embodied dual-consciousness.

Cochrane's objections to alien sex evaporate when he sees his Companion in the form of a lovely woman. Now that she has human flesh, he reciprocates her affections fully. Incarnation has, however, robbed her of her immortality, or the ability to bestow it on Cochrane. She has 'given up everything to be human', but as far as *Star Trek* is concerned that's worth any price. Because the Companion would die if she left the planet of her origin, she expects her time with Cochrane to be brief, as he will fly off in the shuttle to do more boldly going. Yet, much as he hungered to do that previously, the presence of a human companion and, though it's unspoken, suitable sexual partner suffices. Cochrane asks to be left behind to live out a mortal life with the Hedford hybrid, his continued survival kept secret. His life has been extended beyond its intended duration. He has already accomplished much. For this limited second act, his work to grow his own food and tend his vine and fig tree will count as striving enough.

Defying the limitations the universe sets on individual and cultural lifespans receives a thorough critique in 'Return to Tomorrow'. Travelling hundreds of light years beyond any previous exploration by Earth vessels, the *Enterprise* encounters all that's left of a great humanoid species whose planet's surface has been dead for half a million years: the preserved consciousnesses of three of their number. These beings had colonised much of the galaxy, and their leader, Sargon (James Doohan), calls the crew 'my children'. They brought a great cataclysm upon themselves, leading Kirk to mention his planet's own survival of its nuclear age. Sargon dismisses this minor achievement. 'There comes to all races an ultimate crisis which you have yet to face,' he says. His people gained such superior powers of mind that they thought themselves gods and, when they turned on each other, they destroyed their civilisation. Sargon hopes to begin again by installing his mind, that of his wife Thalassa and of Henoch, from the 'other' side, into android bodies. They simply need to borrow three of the crew's bodies for however long it takes to construct their new cybernetic homes.

True to *Star Trek*'s valorisation of the flesh, first Henoch and then Thalassa realise that life in anything besides an organic body is not worth living and they hope to convince Sargon to let them keep the bodies of Spock, Lt Ann Mulhall (Diana Muldaur) and James Kirk. Unlike the dying Nancy Hedford, who retains her selfhood in the lifesaving merger with the Companion, these individuals would be effectively erased in order to provide sensate incarnation for the powerful alien intelligences. Sargon had hoped to live among humanoids, 'teaching them, helping them not to make the errors we did'. But he concludes that fleshly desires and highly evolved brains are never a safe combination. After tricking the devilish Henoch to abandon

Spock, Sargon restores the crews' minds to their bodies and decides that he and Thalassa will consign themselves to oblivion, much as the 'gods' did in 'Who Mourns for Adonais?'. As Sargon's children, humans seem likely to recapitulate their ancestors' history: an evolution that brings many wondrous achievements but eventually goes too far and must succumb to extinction. *Star Trek*'s humanism is just as much essentialist as ideological. To be a consciousness embodied in flesh is the only truly meaningful way to live, even if that dooms individual lives to relatively short duration and requires constant vigilance if the species is not to lapse into predatorial blood lust. Let mind far outstrip body, and the result is either incorporeality become sterile and tyrannical or incarnated power so great that it destroys. Eschew natural evolution, however, and stagnant regression ensues. The show endorses a near future in which man is approaching the best he will be before the downward half of his evolution begins. Yet there's never a point where perfection results. Human beings will forever be on this side of paradise, a fate that Kirk accepts with equanimity. As he corrects the immortal Flint's (James Daly) despair about humankind's inherent depravity in 'Requiem for Methuselah',

> Those pressures are everywhere, in everyone, urging him to what you call savagery; the private hells, the inner needs and mysteries, the beast of instinct. As human beings, that is the way it is; to be human is to be complex. You can't avoid a little ugliness, from within and from without.

3 *Star Trek: The Next Generation*: The Best of Both Worlds

Twenty years of groping to prove the things I'd done before were not accidents.

Dr Richard Daystrom, *Star Trek* 'The Ultimate Computer'

Like Dr Daystrom, whose duotronic computer operating system had revolutionised cybernetics, Gene Roddenberry and his collaborators had revolutionised television science fiction and its fandom. Yet twenty years later *Star Trek* remained Roddenberry's most recent success. Several of his other science-fiction television pilots had not sold and his performance as producer of *Star Trek: The Motion Picture* (1979) had so displeased Paramount that they transferred supervision of the subsequent films to Harve Bennett, despite *Star Trek: The Motion Picture*'s financial success. But in 1986 Roddenberry got another chance when the studio approved a second *Trek* series, which he would eventually decide to situate seventy-five years after the end of the original, with a completely new cast and a ship, the *Enterprise-D*, which would be the fourth successor to the NCC 1701.

Unfortunately, also like Dr Daystrom, Roddenberry's need to validate his position as the genius behind the *Trek* universe was accompanied by emotional instability and paranoia that alienated most

The *Enterprise-D*

of the staff he had assembled to help him create the show. As D. C. Fontana describes the situation:

> No one but Gene could be recognized as a contributor to ideas for the show. No one else could write a final draft. Writer-producers on the series felt the same anger and outrage I did at being excluded from the production process; at being told not to visit the sets or speak to the actors; at watching perfectly good scripts being rewritten by Gene into something far less . . . In the space of nine months, no fewer than eight writing-staff members left the series. . . . A twenty-four year friendship and a lot of respect died during that long summer. I turned my back on Gene Roddenberry and *Star Trek* and walked away.[26]

59

However, unlike Daystrom's M-5 unit, whose creator's instability led to a desire for extinction, *TNG* survived the defections of all the original series' personnel who had developed the show's concept (Fontana, David Gerrold, Bob Justman, Eddie Milkis), a revolving door that saw twenty-four staff writers and writer-producers come and go in three years, and a Writers' Guild of America strike during 1988, which necessitated a twenty-two-episode second season and the adaptation of scripts first developed for the abortive 'Star Trek Phase II' series, which was abandoned to film *Star Trek: The Motion Picture*. By the end of its seven-year run *TNG* would become the most successful of all the *Star Trek* series.[27]

Paramount's liaison, producer Rick Berman, eventually gained enough of Roddenberry's trust to persuade him to withdraw from his disruptive hands-on control of the writing and revision process. By the beginning of the third season, Berman and the head writer he had hired that year, Michael Piller, had de facto control of the show. Over the next three years they would assemble a nucleus of staff writers who would remain with the franchise into the runs of *DS9* and *Voyager*: Jeri Taylor, Ron Moore, Joe Menosky, Brannon Braga and René Echevarria. Despite this continuity, each of the spinoff shows would have its own, distinct identity, just as *TNG* would make considerable changes to the role of the *Enterprise* in the *Trek* universe.

The Board of Directors

The character ensemble featured in *TNG* would differ from that of *Star Trek* in a number of ways. It split the 'Kirk-function' between the captain, Jean-Luc Picard (Patrick Stewart), and the first officer, William T. Riker (Jonathan Frakes). Riker would be the American ladies' man, the action hero, the officer who operated on instinct and adrenaline and went on away missions while the captain stayed on board. He hosts off-duty poker games and excels at bluffing. Picard, on the other hand, is a reflective, cerebral, disciplined and private Frenchman with a British accent, always positioned as aloof from the group socialising of the crew. When an alien imposter takes his place in 'Allegiance', the crew sees through the deception as soon as he shows up in the Ten Forward bar, buys everyone drinks and starts singing. Indeed, although the android Data inherits Spock's lack of emotions, tendency towards encyclopedic accuracy and status as outsider commenting on humanity, a good case can be made that *TNG* put a near-Vulcan in the captain's chair. Picard wins the trust and admiration of Spock's estranged father, Sarek, and eventually mind-melds with him. When Spock meets Picard in 'Unification' (Part 2) he is struck by how much the human resembles his Vulcan parent.

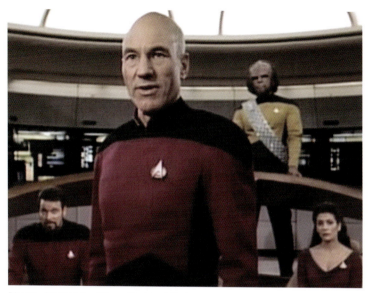

Picard, flanked by Riker, Worf and Troi

61

The bifurcation of the command structure between Picard and Riker divides the cast into two contrasting but parallel groups along an intuitive/empirical axis, which mimics the chief ontological questions of *Star Trek*. Neither the captain nor 'Number One' represents a synthesis of the two problem-solving methods in the way that Captain Kirk did. Decisions are always a matter of negotiation and complementarity between them and their surrogates. Roddenberry had decided that, a generation later, Starfleet officers would be above petty, personal bickering, so however intense the disagreements on principles, the losers blend seamlessly into the overall team once there is a plan to be carried out, fitting for an ensemble drama not featuring its star every week.

Picard heads the empiricists. He rarely has facts and solutions directly to hand, instead commanding by soliciting opinions, choosing which option to follow and then delegating its implementation with his catch-phrase 'Make it so'. Although a social scientist and humanist by training, anthropology and Shakespeare being twin passions, his most frequent personal interactions are with crew members belonging to the science and engineering teams, rather than with fellow command officers. Picard relies on Data for the bulk of his information, and he in turn mentors the android in his quest to understand what it means to be human. He has a similar relationship with teenaged science prodigy Wesley Crusher (Wil Wheaton) and a quasi-romantic friendship of long standing with Wesley's mother Beverly Crusher (Gates McFadden), the ship's chief medical officer. Data's best friend among the crew is his own doctor, the chief engineer Geordi La Forge (LeVar Burton), who often helps carry out Data's scientific and technological remedies when the ship is in danger.

The captain is also especially likely to come to the defence of inorganic beings and non-humanoid aliens. His magnificent defence of Data's 'human rights' in 'The Measure of a Man' set the stage for his championing the self-determination of the 'microbrains' threatened by terra-forming in 'Home Soil', the evolving nanites in 'Evolution', the exocomp robots in 'The Quality of Life' and even the deadly crystalline entity that had wiped out the populations of a number of planets ('Silicon Avatar').

Riker, as the leader of the away team, has to specialise in confronting problems with other beings, rather than with policy or technology. He is more likely to be drawn emotionally to aliens, or to become angered by them, than the dispassionate Picard. He works most closely with security chief Worf, whose Klingon aggressiveness is a *reductio ad absurdum* of Riker's occasional hot temper just as Data's encyclopedic monologues and lack of feelings serve to exaggerate Picard's cerebral and guarded disposition.

Just as Picard does with Dr Crusher, Riker has a long-standing relationship with a female member of the command staff, Counselor Deanna Troi (Marina Sirtis). Troi, an empathic half-Betazoid, is in charge of the crew's emotional health. Like Riker she tends to dominate storylines involving romance, passion and sexuality, and for five and a half seasons she inexplicably wore non-standard uniforms that accentuated her cleavage. Whereas the friendship between Picard and

Dr Crusher has elements of sexual attraction that neither has ever acted upon, Riker and Troi had been passionate lovers some years before, only to part over career issues.

To have the captain of the ship on one side of such a set of binary oppositions presents a practical problem in regard to the command decisions he makes. A lack of 'people skills' is not the best qualification for a leadership position. *TNG* resolves this dilemma by having Troi serve as a link between Picard's intellectual and scientific advisers and the more passionate field operatives. She even has a seat on the bridge so that she can read the emotional nuances of potential adversaries for her emotionally tone-deaf captain.

The many briefings held in the observation lounge give the writers an opportunity to place various attitudes towards morally complex issues in the mouths of the command ensemble. An archetypal *TNG* moment comes in 'Q Who?' when the first word out of Picard's mouth after the crew has narrowly escaped destruction in their first encounter with a Borg cube is 'Conference!' Yet, over time, the trademark conference scenes make it clear that Picard is less likely to rely on the gut instincts of Riker, Troi or Worf than to adopt the more scientific remedies offered by Data, Crusher or La Forge. This tendency actually becomes a crucial plot point in the episode 'Cause and Effect'. The *Enterprise* finds itself trapped in a temporal causality loop that has resulted from a collision with another Starfleet vessel within a rupture in the space-time continuum. Each time the potential collision nears, Picard asks for suggestions to avoid it. Riker proposes that they decompress the main shuttlebay because the explosion might alter their course sufficiently to avert disaster. Data believes that the better solution is to engage the tractor beam to deflect the other vessel. Every time, Picard authorises Data to implement his plan. Every time, they blow up. Only when Data receives the subliminal message he sent himself on the previous iteration of the loop, telling him to use Riker's method instead, do both ships escape the loop.

Data's assumption of the 'outlier position' serves many of the same narrative functions as did Spock's. Just as Spock's having green

63

Lt Commander Data

blood, enhanced strength and mental discipline often made him immune to biological threats that incapacitate the human crew, so Data's being of cybernetic origin allows him to accomplish tasks that no creature of flesh and blood could either perform or survive. Both are on the receiving end of human bigotry. Nevertheless, the critique of humanity that Spock provides is more or less absent. Whereas Spock strives to repress his humanity in favour of the Vulcan logic he never ceases to believe superior, Data yearns from the beginning to be human. There is no more sincere cheerleader for the virtues of humanity than Data, even if he is sometimes used to raise questions about those times in which human beings do not live up to their best selves. The writers arranged an onscreen conversation between Data and Spock in 'Unification' (Part 2) to make overt their contrasting attitudes to the humanity the one seeks to disavow and the other longs to possess. When Spock notes enviously, 'You have an efficient intellect, superior physical skills, no emotional impediments. There are Vulcans who aspire all their lives to achieve what you've been given by design,' Data responds, 'You are half human. . . . Yet you have chosen a Vulcan way of life. . . . In effect you have abandoned what I have sought all *my* life.'

Utopia Comes Early

Many of *TNG*'s broad thematic concerns likewise depart from the preoccupations of the original series. Federation diplomats were necessary evils there, but here conflict resolution and mediation dominate many missions. Plots concern the finer points of intergalactic law and treaty negotiations and the importance of precision in communication among different species. This in turn leads to an emphasis on how one culture reads another. In place of the rigid distinction between living organism and sterile mechanism of its predecessor, *TNG* often conflates the two. With consciousness valued without regard to its embodiment, threats to consciousness became paramount. The change that most differentiates *TNG* from its predecessor, however, involves its elevated view of what it means to serve in Starfleet.

65

Although *Star Trek* asserts that humankind can overcome its destructive ways to avoid annihilation and join with other species in friendship, Kirk and his crew display many flaws; truly evolved aliens see them as fractious but promising children who might grow up to be all right at some point in the far future. On the *Enterprise-D*, however, the maturation process seems to have accelerated a hundredfold. The crew are paragons of professional competence and lofty ideals. As Steven F. Collins notes: 'From the first episode, *TNG* established a view of itself as already-actualized perfected liberalism.'[28] When the magisterial Picard has a talk with more quarrelsome species or individuals, he sounds a lot like a Metron or an Organian putting a hubristic Kirk in his place.

As noted above, Roddenberry felt that he had a responsibility to all those fans who read utopian hopes into the original series to show those hopes coming to fruition. Second, the late 80s and early 90s were a time when it briefly looked possible that the world was entering a new era of peace and cooperation. Reagan and Gorbachev signed arms reduction treaties in the year *TNG* debuted. In 1989 the Soviet Empire collapsed, symbolised by the fall of the Berlin Wall. In August 1991, at nearly the same time that Gene Roddenberry died, the Soviet Union disbanded and the Cold War ended. Politicians envisioned a 'New World Order'. Francis Fukuyama was persuaded – quite prematurely, it turned out – to declare the end of history in 1992.[29]

With the Cold War that had been the template for *Star Trek*'s galactic politics over, *TNG* imagines a universe in which the Federation is no longer involved in struggles among the great Alpha Quadrant powers, even though the Romulans did emerge from self-imposed seclusion to keep Starfleet on its toes. New foes are the goblin-like Ferengi, rampant capitalists who personify 80s greed but come across as grotesque comic figures more laughable than threatening. The Borg deal the Federation a horrific, crippling blow in 'The Best of Both Worlds', but they retreat after appearing in only three other episodes. The spacecraft is more focused on statecraft, with many episodes devoted to Picard directly or indirectly helping to mediate local conflicts. Even more important to Federation equilibrium in the twenty-fourth century, however, is the end of the struggle for natural resources that often occupied the first *Enterprise* crew when something happened to its dilithium crystals. The invention of the replicator creates a post-scarcity economy.

The replicator, like the holodeck that figures prominently in the first hour of 'Encounter at Farpoint', turns energy into matter. It seems a likely advance on the technology of the transporter, which converts matter into a data stream and then reconstitutes it somewhere else. The added benefit of the holodeck and replicator is that they don't have to start with existing matter. The energy itself, shaped by a digital algorithm, can magically become food that nourishes or weapons that kill, a landscape distant in time and place or a lover who provides guilt-free pleasures. While the writers are always hazy on why whatever provides the energy to fuel replicators is cheap and abundant, the fact that the replicator leads to a Federation where citizens can have whatever they need, work at whatever fulfils them and abandon a monetary economy tells us that it is so plentiful and accessible as to be of negligible concern. Replicators seem an even more insidious way to castrate the will than the paternalism of all those super-computers Kirk destroyed so that humanoids could learn the value of struggle and striving, but apparently Picard's ability to make 'Tea. Earl Grey. Hot' materialise out of thin air threatens the next generation no more than his having an android as his operations officer.

Dealings with other life forms undergo the same sorts of shifts relative to the original series. In *Star Trek*, despite the Prime Directive, Kirk never hesitated to destroy the status quo on planets whose populations were endangered by tyranny or war. At the same time, the Federation was always eager for allies and trading partners, so that a society only had to be trying to evolve to earn the sometimes dubious gift of Starfleet experts on the ground and Federation membership in the future. This parallels the US Cold War struggles to keep developing and emerging nations from falling to communism, and looking the other way at how leaders of these allies treated their own people. Kirk's foreign policy might be dubbed 'coercive inclusiveness'.

Picard's policies, by contrast, can be dubbed 'condescending exclusiveness'. 'Enterprise crewmembers let Others know that they are inherently inferior and that they should act more like Enterprise crewmembers, who embody ideal human potential,' Kent Ono points out.[30] Thus, not just anyone can get into the twenty-fourth-century Federation. Several episodes ('Manhunt', 'The Hunted', 'Attached') deal with planets whose applications the *Enterprise* crew considers and rejects. Even with planets that have made no overtures to the Federation, indeed sometimes with aliens who belong to the Federation, there is more often than not a sense that Picard has judged them and found them wanting. (Patrick Stewart developed an acting mannerism associated with scenes in which the captain had to explain some Starfleet verity that a less ethically discriminating listener could not grasp. He would pause, sigh heavily, and then deliver his peroration.) Often not overt, this disdain comes through in the number of episodes in which the *Enterprise* is on hand to help an alien scientist with an important technological breakthrough that never quite comes off, in contrast to the desperate, improvised tech fixes Data and La Forge devise during crises, which never fail to work perfectly. Especially in the earlier seasons, Federation member species would come aboard the *Enterprise* and antagonise everyone by unseemly displays of arrogance or rigidity in doing things only as they are done in the native culture.

At the same time, *TNG*'s Federation rarely intercedes to force the aliens to conform to its values and cultural practices. At most there will be a lecture on current failings and an action plan suggested, should the population want to improve itself. If one of his other officers expresses frustration that the crew will not put an end to behaviours perceived as barbaric, Picard will caution that others must be taken as we find them. When his own security officer, Worf, insists on committing ritual suicide rather than live with paralysis, which is the Klingon way, Dr Crusher is furious, but Picard understands completely:

> Beverly, he cannot make the journey you are asking of him. You want him to go from contemplating suicide to accepting his condition and living with a disability. But it's too far, and the road between covers a lifetime of values and beliefs. He cannot do it.

I've always thought that Picard's position could best be summed up by the epigram 'We absolutely defend your right to be wrong.' This is the paradox, perhaps, that causes many scholars to find *TNG* neoconservative in its attitudes[31] while many internet fans complain that it is 'too PC'.

The perfect episode to illustrate this dictum is 'First Contact', which reveals, step-by-step, how the Federation approaches a species on the verge of warp capability and interstellar travel. It begins in a hospital emergency room where obvious aliens treat a man who has been injured in a violent demonstration. The patient is soon revealed to be Commander Riker, surgically altered to resemble the aliens, known as

Malcorians. Riker's injury exposes an aspect of Federation first contact protocols that Starfleet does not usually foreground: to prepare the way for the initial encounter, experts conduct the euphemistically named 'surface reconnaissance'. That is, they plant undercover operatives on a targeted planet for years. This is apparently only the final stage of extensive Federation surveillance of all the pre-warp civilisations in the quadrant, because they monitor broadcasts and activity in local space in order to know when the time is right to send in the reconnaissance teams and who would be the ideal planetary inhabitant to approach first. Picard and Troi beam down to discuss the situation with Mirasta Yale (Carolyn Seymour), the lead researcher for the Malcorian warp programme. Picard reassuringly explains their *modus operandi*, which reveals that the Federation shares his own preference for empiricism: 'We prefer meeting like this rather than a random confrontation in deep space. We've come to you because you are a leader in the scientific community. Scientists generally accept our arrival more easily than others.'

Scientist Yale and Chancellor Durken

The rest of the episode deals with determining what the attitudes of the rest of the population might be to the revelation that they are not the sole sentient beings in the universe, as they believe, but merely 'one voice in a chorus'. A continuum exists among those who learn of the human visitors, and it is played out, on the one hand, in the halls of power, between Yale, the progressive but cautious Chancellor Durken (George Coe) and the mistrustful chief of security and defender of 'traditional' values, Krola (Michael Ensign); and on the other, among the hospital staff. A quirky female UFO enthusiast, Lanel (Bebe Neuwirth), a parody of Yale's life-long dream of flying to the stars, agrees to help Riker if he sleeps with her; the prudent head administrator, Berel (George Hearn), wishes to keep the whole matter quiet but will not, on principle, allow harm to come to Riker; and the paranoid doctor Nilrem (Steven Anderson) starts rumours that the Malcorian space flights have attracted the attention of dangerous invaders. Eventually the revelation of the covert intelligence-gathering and Krola's willingness to die rather than permit a Starfleet presence nullify Durken's initial inclination to let the Federation 'guide [Malcor] into a new era'. He decides to slow down his forward-looking agenda, cancel the warp programme and devote more time to educating his people so that they will be ready to accept the existence of humanoid life elsewhere in the galaxy. Picard regrets the lost opportunity but departs as asked, without feeling any Kirkian temptation to destroy the planet's infrastructure so that it will wake up to the superiority of the Federation way of life.

Durken and Picard do agree to let Yale leave on the *Enterprise* and so see the wider galaxy that would otherwise be closed to her during her lifetime, while the Malcorians slowly shed enough tradition and 'sweet innocence' to accept their diminished place in the universe. As long as a culture produces individuals open to new experiences like Yale and can some day transcend superstition and tradition, they can grow into Utopia, even if it must be deferred while ideological stragglers are brought up to speed. Malcor is, in fact, quite obviously a send-up of the Earth of the early 90s and the writers have no desire to tell the audience that they won't ever measure up to the shining example of twenty-fourth-century humans.

Barclay, confident on the holodeck

As a counter to the formidable self-assurance of the *Enterprise* 71
crew in the face of the manifold failings of people who don't meet their
standards, the writers did introduce an officer who isn't a model of
perfection. Diagnostic engineer Lt Reg Barclay (Dwight Schultz) is shy,
nervous and lacks self-confidence, hiding in an alternate ship on the
holodeck where he can feel safe and powerful amid caricatures of his
fellow officers. Riker tells Picard that 'the question is whether Mr
Barclay is *Enterprise* material'. La Forge adds that 'I can barely tolerate
being in the same room with the man', and, when ordered to mentor
him, insists to a Guinan more sympathetic to Barclay's plight that 'he
just doesn't fit in here'. The contemptuous nickname 'Broccoli' even
slips out of the mouth of Picard, who otherwise defends the misfit's
expertise and devotion to duty. But Barclay's out-of-the-box thinking
proves invaluable on several occasions. Although never cured of his
social awkwardness and phobias, he became a favourite recurring
character. He appears in five *TNG* episodes, the film *Star Trek: First
Contact* and in seven *Voyager* episodes as well.

You Speak the Language of Diplomacy Well

This section's sub-heading quotes Chancellor Durken's reply to Picard after listening to his initial presentation urging first contact with the Federation. Durken adds that the language of diplomacy can often mask dangers. In its many episodes that focus upon all sorts of negotiations, *TNG* demonstrates that the language of diplomacy can indeed accompany serious threats, even of death or physical harm, although less often to the other party than to the negotiator himself.

Two early episodes in which the *Enterprise* escorts famed mediators to troublespots highlight this theme. In 'Too Short a Season' ailing octogenarian Admiral Mark Jameson (Clayton Rohner) returns to a planet where he tried to broker a peace agreement forty-five years before. Karnas (Michael Pataki), one of the parties to that failed negotiation, has taken Federation personnel hostage as a ploy, it turns out, to lure Jameson there and kill him. It is revealed that Jameson might have brokered a peace the first time around, but instead authorised the arming of both disputatious parties. Karnas has recently emerged the Pyrrhic victor of the devastating civil war that ensued. Jameson feels so guilty that in order to make amends by getting the hostages released, he takes an overdose of an experimental drug that makes him grow younger and younger but ultimately results in his painful death. Karnas realises that Jameson has, in effect, enacted his revenge for him, and he and Picard manage to negotiate an end to the crisis.

'Loud as a Whisper' features another diplomatic legend, Riva (Howie Seago). The royal family on his planet, to which he belongs, lacks the gene for hearing and speech; Riva reads lips but has a 'chorus' of assistants who telepathically comprehend his thoughts and moods and speak the words he uses in his diplomacy. A bit too self-assured as to his skills and his reputation, Riva doesn't take sufficient precautions upon his first meeting with representatives of the two warring factions on a planet that has been embroiled in strife for centuries. One man disagrees with the decision to try to make peace and opens fire, killing all the members of the chorus. Unable to be understood himself now,

Riva and his chorus

73

Riva loses all confidence and wants to abandon the peace talks, but he eventually realises that he can teach sign language to all the parties involved, and their learning to communicate in this new way can help them to get past the points of conflict that are so ingrained in their thinking.

The often high cost of negotiations might lead the audience to wonder whether *TNG* is not as committed to talking one's way through conflicts as it seems to be. Dramatic considerations, however, are probably more responsible for this repeated theme. A few disastrous setbacks are necessary to render discussions around a conference table suspenseful and propel the plot along. Moreover, the sacrifices often demanded reinforce the series' insistence that dying heroically for peace trumps dying heroically in war.

If understanding other cultures broadly is a prerequisite for successful negotiations, understanding their words precisely is just as essential. Picard's abilities to comprehend the nuances of what is said to him and to traverse the fine points of words codified into law are important enough to earn attention in several episodes as well. The through-line from anthropology to linguistics is traced brilliantly in one of *TNG*'s best, 'Darmok'. Richards, indeed, finds it 'the finest episode of the series', exemplifying how *Trek* 'sees myth as performing a vital and underappreciated function: as the central means of communication between races and as the very basis of language itself'.[32] The dilemma facing the crew arises from an encounter with the Tamarians. Although the universal translator renders the Tamarian language into English vocabulary and syntax, its semantics make no sense to outsiders. Suddenly, in an apparently hostile action, they beam Picard and their captain, Dathon (Paul Winfield), down to the planet El-Adrel, which both ships are orbiting. The events on the planet slowly reveal to Picard (and in parallel to Data and Troi on the *Enterprise*) that the Tamarian language is exclusively allusive and metaphoric, with the referent for each metaphor being one of the great heroic myths of the Tamarian people. Wishing to end his people's incomprehensibility to others, Dathon has taken the great gamble (which costs him his life) of re-enacting with his human counterpart a key battle from one of those epics in order to create the beginnings of a shared frame of reference. At the same time, a new myth is established of Picard and Dathon at El-Adrel, one which can enlarge the Tamarian language's store of metaphor.

In the end, though, 'Darmok' stresses the importance of a shared mythic heritage for any given culture rather than an exchange of mythic referents across cultures. Picard tells the dying Dathon the story of Gilgamesh and later is seen brushing up on the Homeric epics. Unspoken in this evocation of texts that are regrettably now high cultural arcana for most of the *TNG* audience is the suggestion that popular culture, too, can provide unifying metaphors, as *Trek* has surely done.

The primacy placed on negotiating in many episodes minimises the fact that once negotiations have succeeded, language is codified into laws, treaties and contracts, which may become rigid and betray the

Dathon and Picard

original goal of mutual benefits that inspired them. 'The Ensigns of Command' addresses the issue head on. An advanced, non-humanoid species called the Sheliak grudgingly learns several Federation languages in order to negotiate a treaty clearly demarcating their territory, but that having happened, communication with the lower forms of life they consider humanoids to be no longer interests them. They break a 111-year silence when they discover that a planet they claim and are about to colonise is occupied by human survivors of a wrecked transport who had intended to settle elsewhere. Picard agrees to evacuate the trespassers, even though they are none too eager to give up the life they have carved out of the harsh conditions, but the Sheliak, going by the letter of the 500,000-word treaty they demanded because they find the Federation languages 'irrational', refuse to grant the extension in the time necessary to assemble enough transports to remove the colonists. The Sheliak vow to exterminate the human 'vermin' if they arrive to find them still in residence. After much research into the treaty's text, Picard hoists them on their own petard: one codicil of the treaty allows either party to call for third-party arbitration at any time. He selects a species currently in hibernation, a gambit that makes the Sheliak finally agree to some flexibility, since a three-week extension of the treaty provision beats the six months it will take for the arbitration to occur.

Picard is never as hung up on the letter rather than the spirit of the law as are the Sheliak, but he does lean towards legalistic solutions, even when they threaten to imperil innocents. (Kirk would have defended the rights of the human colonists to remain, convincing the Sheliak that the two communities could coexist, and meeting any extermination threats with a few photon torpedo blasts.) Although circumstances allow for their eventual salvation, he lets the Prime Directive give him pause before rescuing Wesley from a death sentence for, essentially, not keeping off the grass in 'Justice'; is ready to leave Sarjenka (Nikki Cox) and her planet to its fate in 'Pen Pals'; and, in 'Homeward', allows the majority of the population of Boraal II to perish rather than reveal the existence of aliens and space travel to the primitive inhabitants. He confesses to Ensign Ro (Michelle Forbes) that Federation protocols against interference in species' internal affairs led it to stand by as the Cardassians occupied Bajor and displaced or exterminated its people. The increased seriousness with which the Prime Directive and other laws are viewed in *TNG* does eliminate the frequent *Star Trek* scenario of Kirk destroying the source of a planet's entire infrastructure and then leaving the inhabitants with an admonition to become self-reliant, but it also permits the crew to stand by and do nothing when people who have the misfortune not yet to have achieved travel into deep space are desperate for their aid.

Domestic Space

On both seafaring and spacefaring vessels of our own time, private space is at a premium. *Star Trek*'s *Enterprise* wasn't particularly cramped or spartan, but neither were crew quarters and recreational spaces luxurious. The *Enterprise-D*, on the other hand, resembles an upmarket cruise ship more than a military vessel. When Scotty is brought out of seventy-five years of suspended animation and assigned ordinary crew quarters there, he's sure he must have displaced the captain and been given his lavish suite. As the only starship in the franchise with a substantial civilian complement, the *Enterprise-D* has to serve as communal space for families and auxiliary service personnel at the same time that it fulfils its military, research and technological functions. In addition to laboratories, engineering centres, cargo bays and briefing rooms, there is a school, the holodeck and various performance spaces. Crew give concerts, stage plays and teach Klingon martial arts. Children compete in a science fair. All these amenities are meant to obviate the difficulty stated a number of times in the original series: signing on as a career Starfleet officer virtually guarantees impermanent romantic relationships and estrangement from family.

Paradoxically, the elimination of obstacles to being with family means little to the regular ensemble because their own families are more burden than blessing. Richards notes the unmarried and childless state of most of the principals (Crusher and later Worf are single parents). Moreover, when parents or siblings come to visit 'no crew member is ever glad to receive [them] on board. . . . The typical visiting family member is well intentioned, self-absorbed, and meddlesome.' He denominates Troi's free-spirited, sex-starved and embarrassingly candid mother Lwaxana (Majel Barrett) as the archetypal unwanted relative: 'Part of space exploration in *Star Trek* seems to involve getting away from family members like Lwaxana Troi.'[33] (A counter-argument can be made, I think, that the writers use Lwaxana, like the equally aggravating Q (John de Lancie), to poke fun at the stuffy, way-too-serious Starfleeters demanded by Roddenberry's requirements for more exemplary Federation citizens.)

If the families they come from can irritate the characters, the children they can't have or can't keep are cause for sorrow ('The Child', 'The Offspring'). The concept of unfulfilled parenthood is explored most insistently with Picard. From the pilot on, his discomfort around children

77

Lwaxana Troi

is pointed up, while at the same time his abjuration of fatherhood is called into question. Wesley tells him flat out that it's a shame he never chose to be a father, because he would have been a good one ('Samaritan Snare'). He's the only father-figure to whom Jono (Chad Allen), a human boy raised by warlike aliens, will listen ('Suddenly Human'). But Picard can't be a biological father for the simple reason that his role requires him to be a symbolic father, to articulate what Jacques Lacan calls 'the Law of the Father'. As Ilsa Bick has perceptively argued, there's something about these Starfleet crews of the eternal pre-Oedipal child.[34] As long as Picard stands in for the concept of an all-wise and beneficent father, there's no need for them to overcome their real fathers and move on with their lives into more adult personal relationships.

This is never more apparent than in the Picard–Riker relationship. Riker is by all accounts an accomplished officer, entering into mid-career, and yet he remains second in command, not because no one offers him a ship of his own but because he keeps turning down such offers. On one such occasion his father, Kyle (Mitchell Ryan), visits to try to persuade him to leave the *Enterprise* for command of another vessel. The two have a strained relationship, and we find out that Will has never been able to defeat his father at the game of paresi squares, a metaphor of his failed Oedipalisation. What's worse, Kyle has stymied his son's normal psychic development by cheating in order to remain undefeated. In the end, it is apparent that because his biological father is so sorely lacking, Riker would rather not challenge the authority of the ideal father whom Picard represents. The writers try to make this issue go away in 'The Best of Both Worlds' (Parts 1 and 2). Riker has once again been offered a captaincy, and an ambitious officer, Elizabeth Shelby (Elizabeth Dennehy), is gunning to replace him on the *Enterprise*. Once again Riker is not disposed to accept the offer, but all this politics becomes moot when the ship encounters the Borg, who kidnap and assimilate Picard, designating him as Locutus, their spokesman. When Riker gives the order to fire upon the Borg cube containing Locutus, he appears to have gained his Oedipal triumph as the first part ends on *Trek*'s most famous cliffhanger. Yet the Borg vessel and Picard/Locutus, of course, aren't destroyed, and Riker sits in the captain's ready room plagued by doubts as to his fitness to do what Picard would have done in his place. Bringing him out of his funk takes a lecture from Guinan, of all people, who tells him that he has to think for himself and implement his own strategy to save Earth from the Borg, who have crippled the *Enterprise* and destroyed the Federation fleet at Wolf 359. And yet Riker's triumph depends upon retrieving Picard and using his connection to the Borg to incapacitate them; it is even Picard, still half-assimilated, who comes up with the perfect command to get the job done: tell all the drones to 'go to sleep'.

79

Breaches, Rifts and Ruptures

If the vulnerability most stressed in *Star Trek* is a danger of depletion, loss of energy, decay of orbits, that of *TNG* is of infiltration, invasion, infection, something from the outside getting in, just the strategy which knocks out that Borg cube. At one extreme, rifts and breaches that bring together alternative universes have potentially disastrous consequences. In 'Yesterday's Enterprise' Picard's crew undergoes a sinister transformation when a rift in the space-time continuum lets through an *Enterprise* of twenty years earlier, the 1701-C, which was destroyed in a battle between the Klingons and the Romulans. By coming to the aid of the beleaguered Klingons, the 1701-C helped pave the way for peace between them and the Federation. With the ship now stuck in the future, that future itself has changed, with Starfleet on a constant war footing, its utopian missions of diplomacy and research cast aside. History is restored by sending the 1701-C back through the rift, its crew willing to give up their lives to preserve peace, and then sealing the rift. In 'Schisms' one of La Forge's experiments involving tetryons allows aliens who live in subspace to kidnap crew members and perform invasive and horrific medical experiments on them. *TNG*'s two-hour series finale, 'All Good Things . . .', also uses this device. Here an anomaly in space-time is created by attempts to destroy it (don't ask) and, if not diffused, the anomaly will prevent the evolution of life on Earth from occurring. With Q's help, a Picard jumping through time manages to solve the puzzle and determine the solution.

Sometimes the ruptures are on a smaller scale than between regions of space or alternate universes. Nanites Wesley modified as a science experiment evolve and infest the ship's systems in 'Evolution'; Data's puzzling dreams, when decoded, reveal that interphasic parasites are eating away the cellular peptides in the makeup of both ship and crew in 'Phantasms'. A virulent space bacterium starts eroding the hulls of the *Enterprise* and a Klingon vessel on which Riker is serving as part of a cultural exchange in 'A Matter of Honor'. The emphasis on disease-like organisms infecting systems or eating through exteriors may reflect *TNG*'s initial broadcasts during the height of the AIDS epidemic, although in each case the infections first get into starships and not into bodies. (Even the provocatively titled 'Contagion' is about a computer virus and not a pathogen.) Such displacements reveal how the bodies of the *Enterprise* crew and the body of the ship itself are seen as interchangeable and continuous in the series.

Bodies of any sort are never of primary interest on *TNG*, however. The AIDS crisis is far less a subtext than the emotional crises 80s' therapy culture targeted. *TNG* and *Voyager* writer Joe Menosky told Jeff Greenwald, 'When people look back on *Next Gen*, the single thing that will date the show most is *Counselor Troi on the bridge*. That was the embodiment of how far therapy went in the '80s. A therapist was so important, she had to sit next to the captain!'[35] The show returns again and again to interrogating states of consciousness. Specifically it explores how easily consciousness can be altered and perceptions mistaken. When *Star Trek* dealt with such concepts, it was usually very careful to spare the audience from the characters' misapprehensions of reality, but *TNG* many times enjoys fooling the audience into believing that a character's delusions are objective reality.

Particularly vulnerable to psychic invasions are Data and Troi. As an artificial intelligence whose consciousness is contained in a highly sophisticated positronic brain, Data can be 'hacked' by those seeking to control him, as in 'The Schizoid Man' and 'Descent'. As an empath, Troi essentially has an open channel to the thoughts of others and they often overcome the defences of her own self-awareness. In 'Eye of the Beholder' it takes a mere 'empathic residue' of a murder-suicide involving a telepath in a love triangle at the shipyard where the *Enterprise* was built to trigger in Troi and another Betazoid delusions that they are the homicidal and guilt-ridden telepath, casting shipmates in the roles occupied by the original threesome. Other episodes in which Troi gets her consciousness manipulated or hijacked include 'The Loss', 'Man of the People', 'Violations' and 'Night Terrors'. Yet nearly every member of the regular ensemble succumbs at some point. (The cynic in me says that the burden of Roddenberry's dicta about the enlightened way Starfleet officers should behave required these frequent mental takeovers just so the characters could generate some conflict and drama among themselves.)

While the vulnerability of minds and perceptions of reality is the central anxiety of *TNG*, that vulnerability is not uniformly undesirable. There are, to be sure, plenty of sinister mental invasions. In 'Power Play' malevolent spirits banished to a desolate moon take over several crew members, hoping to be freed from their purgatorial existence. In 'Violations' a telepathic historian essentially mind-rapes victims for his own sadistic pleasure. In 'Man of the People' a diplomat's negotiating prowess derives from his dumping all his negative emotions into unwitting female 'receptacles', causing them to age rapidly and die. Aliens often manipulate memories and perceptions because they want the crew to become their instruments, as in 'Clues' and 'Conundrum'. In 'Future Imperfect' a lonely alien boy, desperate for a father, uses his mental powers to convince Riker that sixteen years have passed and that the boy is human and his son.

But sometimes the apparent violations are not meant maliciously, even if they appear to cause harm or even actually do so. They instead represent attempts by alien life forms to communicate, and *TNG* values nothing more highly. In 'The Nth Degree' a curious alien who shares the Federation's zeal to seek out new life and new civilisations but doesn't want to leave home to find them grants Barclay an exponentially expanded intelligence so that he can modify the *Enterprise* to bring it the great distance required to meet the alien. Often the communication is a matter of life and death. For instance, in 'Night Terrors' something is interfering with the crew's REM sleep and ability to dream. This results in hallucinations and paranoia, and the crew deduces that this effect caused thirty-four crew members on a ship adrift in space to kill each other. Neither ship is able to escape the effects because they are being held by one of those pesky spatial rifts, and their impaired mental states prevent them from executing the technological manoeuvre that would free them. For once, Troi is the only crew member not vulnerable; she can dream just fine, but is having nightmares. Because another Betazoid on the doomed ship has also survived, she finally realises that the nightmares are communications sent telepathically from a ship trapped on the other side of the rift. They are jamming the dreaming frequencies of all other humanoid species but broadcasting on the Betazoid wavelength. Troi is able to send instructions through her own dreams to that crew, telling them how to free both ships, and the plan works to create the explosion needed to blast them clear of the rift. In 'Interface' another distress call gets through to La Forge in what appears to be an hallucination of his mother, recently killed on a mission, but is actually a plea from an alien life form trapped on a Federation science vessel. La Forge is interfacing with a probe via his VISOR, with the aim of raising the ship from a planet's turbulent atmosphere. But the aliens have to go lower still in the atmosphere or perish, and by assuming the form of his dead mother, compel La Forge to defy Picard's orders and save their lives.

In two cases long-dead cultures seek to perpetuate a record of themselves by downloading into members of the *Enterprise* crew. Data inadvertently takes on the personalities of numerous archetypal characters from an ancient culture in 'Masks', eventually resulting in a transformation of the *Enterprise* into the site of one of the culture's central myths. Far more benign are the activities of a probe from the extinct Ressikan culture that strikes Picard unconscious and takes over his mind in the beautiful and heartbreaking 'The Inner Light'. Although on one level conscious of his true identity, Picard, under the influence of the probe, assumes the persona of a Ressikan, Kamen, and lives a full life among them, fathering children and grandchildren, using his scientific acumen in an ultimately futile effort to reverse the climate change that will destroy the population. What seems to take decades is accomplished in a few hours and Picard regains consciousness; when he picks up the one physical artefact the probe contains, a flute that Kamen played in the illusory scenario, and can play it as himself as well, the audience knows that the Ressikans will live on as memory.

A slight variation on these 'mind frell' scenarios occurs when the altered reality is generated by characters in order to defend themselves from an outside threat. In 'Frame of Mind' Riker seems to enter the reality of a play he has been rehearsing, in which he portrays a man trapped in a mental hospital. Every time he thinks he has returned to reality, another layer of delusion asserts itself. It is finally revealed

Riker's nightmare
reality

that he has been captured by aliens who are probing his brain, and he
has adapted the dramatic scenario as a way to keep them from accessing
his thoughts. Dr Crusher in 'Remember Me' seems to be the only one on
the ship to notice that crew members keep disappearing. Every time the
ship's complement adjusts downward, those remaining insist that it has
always been so and that sensors show no evidence of mass
disappearances. It turns out that she has been trapped in a warp bubble
and, like Riker, she has interpreted this limbo through the last memories
she made before the accident, speaking with a senior colleague about all
the friends and family he has lost.

Eleventh-Hour Doubts

In 'Emergence', one of the last episodes of the seventh and final season
of *TNG*, many of the threads that run throughout the series join
together: the use of the ship as a metonymy for its inhabitants; of
communication taking place through dreams or hallucinations; and of
the relationships of individuals as members of Starfleet superseding
private familial and affective ties. The story, essentially, concerns the
Enterprise deciding to have a baby. While a bit of a hash dramatically,
this episode serves as a particularly direct articulation of the *TNG*

ideology. A train literally crashing into the holodeck program where Data is rehearsing *The Tempest* with Picard's guidance heralds a series of instances in which the ship locks out the crew and uses its resources to build a mysterious object in the cargo bay. It accomplishes this by manufacturing a sequence of interlinked nodes, which bear a striking resemblance to the structure of the neural nets in both humans' and AIs' brains. The senior staff take this revelation of the *Enterprise*'s 'emergent intelligence' in stride. After all, they say, many ship's functions are analogous to those of biological organisms; its sensors are its eyes, its databases its memories, the holodeck its imagination. Guided by the dream-like images being produced on that holodeck, crew and ship eventually join forces to bring the *Enterprise* to a sufficient source of vertyon particles to enable the cargo bay object to develop a self-generating power source – that is, to come to life. It then exits the ship and flies off into space, after which the emergent intelligence nodes vanish. Picard notes that nature knows of many organisms that live only to procreate and die.

In the episode's coda, Data comes to the captain with doubts. He wonders why Picard did not hesitate to let the new life form be born and enter into the wider galaxy: 'The object could have been dangerous. It may in fact *be* dangerous.' Picard discounts his fears because of the object's parentage:

> The intelligence that was formed on the *Enterprise* didn't just come out of the ship's systems. It came from us, from our mission records, personal logs, holodeck programs – our fantasies. Now, if our experiences with the *Enterprise* have been honourable, can't we trust that the sum of those experiences will be the same?

This statement distills the utopian self-satisfaction that constitutes *TNG*'s portrayal of a future humanity as well as its valuation of the collective being (*pace* Borg) of its crew as equal to, if not preferable to, the atomised and often messy individual relationships that have to be formed and persist in the private activities of partnering and parenting.

The crew ponder the *Enterprise*'s offspring

Nevertheless, several other episodes of that season bring up a counter-discourse. In 'Journey's End', Wesley Crusher, always Picard's symbolic son and heir to the Starfleet tradition, decides to abandon his commission and his career to traverse time and space with the powerful and benevolent alien, the Traveler (Eric Menyuk), who had pegged Wesley as special way back in season one. The occasion of his change of heart is the repetition of a shameful part of human history, the forced relocation of Native Americans from their ancestral lands. Now the admiralty is ordering a planet colonised by those Indians' descendants to be evacuated and ceded to the Cardassians to fulfil a negotiated treaty, like so many of those the *Enterprise* crew has helped facilitate. Wesley takes the side of the colonists and defies his superiors' orders, realising that he isn't meant to be a Starfleet officer when he has a vision of his biological father, who died in the service, telling him to seek a different path. Similarly, in 'Pre-Emptive Strike', Ro Laren, the troubled Bajoran officer whom Picard has given a second chance under his tutelage, is sent undercover to infiltrate the Maquis, a group of Federation terrorists that formed in response to that same ceding of Federation colony worlds to the Cardassians. Instead of bringing about their apprehension, she switches sides and joins their cause, parting from a dismayed Picard, who cannot see things from her perspective and is left feeling bitterly betrayed. Perhaps it is these two incidents, as well as his preview of a

86

bleak, possible post-retirement future in 'All Good Things . . .' that make Picard join in the poker game his senior staff regularly gather for. In doing so, he abdicates his position as symbolic father, bearer of the Law, substituting real, private camaraderie for abstract, public authority. He speaks for himself rather than being the Locutus of Starfleet regulations and the Federation charter. Most importantly, his move suggests that the members of his crew don't need to remain symbolically his children, even as they approach middle age. Like Wesley and Ro Laren, sometimes children must grow up and take different paths than their fathers/mentors have mapped out for them. This would be the ultimate message of *Deep Space Nine*, whose writing staff the authors of 'Journey's End' and 'Pre-Emptive Strike', Ron Moore and René Echevarria respectively, were going off to join.

87

4 *Star Trek: Deep Space Nine*: Necessary Evil

We're not everyone's cup of tea. We're the neurotics' *Star Trek*.

René Auberjonois, Odo on *Deep Space Nine*[36]

The first thing to be said about *DS9* is that it was a vehicle to escape Roddenberry's requirement of a regular cast of Starfleet paragons. 'After years of squeezing the franchise into Roddenberry's conceptual corset, something had to give,' Greenwald writes. '*Deep Space Nine*, created by Berman and Michael Piller in 1991, was the answer. The darker, grittier series, set in a remote space station staffed by wily and rebellious aliens, allows a few lucky writers and producers to let their hair down.'[37] Premiering in January 1993, *DS9* was always intended as a companion show to the franchise's trademark starship sagas; only ten of its 176 episodes aired without competition from *TNG* or *Voyager*. Yet its distinctiveness was not merely for the sake of variety. Especially as executive producer Ira Steven Behr gained more authority over the show's direction in seasons three and four, *DS9* became an outright repudiation of many aspects of *TNG*. 'I did not enjoy writing *TNG*,' he told Terry Erdmann. 'I did not like the lack of conflict, the kind of stodginess, the tech solutions to a lot of problems.'[38] Behr has often said that, as a native of the Bronx, he was always suspicious of the oh-so-genteel residents of the Connecticut suburbs. Picard and crew live in the Federation's Connecticut; Commander, then Captain, Benjamin Sisko

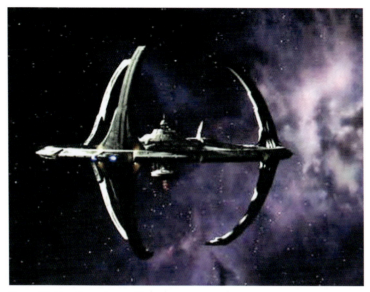

Space Station Deep Space Nine

(Avery Brooks) and the station's motley assemblage in the Bronx. This declaration of difference in fact comes quite early, in the seventh episode, 'Q-Less'. Here Picard's infuriating nemesis is being his usual troublemaking self when he transports himself and Sisko into an early twentieth-century boxing ring. Sisko promptly punches him in the jaw. 'You hit me,' Q whines. 'Picard never hit me!' 'I'm not Picard,' Sisko booms in reply.

The stationary setting of the space station dictated that the characters live with the consequences of their actions rather than flying off on the next mission. Piller explained:

> You create a show about commitment, about the Federation's commitment to Bajor and DS9, about the commitment that people have to make when they go live in a new environment, and have to co-exist with other species who have different agendas than they have. It's like the difference between a one-night stand and a marriage.[39]

That sense of commitment meant that the easily cast-off family member was also a thing of the past. Sisko, the new Federation station commander, is a man still grieving the loss of his wife three years before, an affectionate, demonstrative father to his teenage son Jake (Cirroc Lofton), often hugging and kissing the young man even in later seasons when he grew a head taller than his father. At heart a builder, he likes being settled and domestic and is a wonderful cook, having been schooled by his deeply respected father Joseph (Brock Peters), a prominent New Orleans restaurateur. During the run of the show, Sisko remarries, to freighter captain Kasidy Yates (Penny Johnson), and conceives a second child with her. Two other sets of regular and recurring characters marry (Worf and Jadzia Dax (Terry Farrell), Rom (Max Grodénchik) and Leeta (Chase Masterson)) and Kira (Nana Visitor) and Odo and Bashir (Alexander Siddig) and Ezri Dax (Nicole deBoer) enter into committed relationships.

But wider relationships would resonate throughout the seasons as well. The series had dozens of recurring characters who were indispensable to the unfolding of the stories the regular characters anchored. A number of these frequent guest-starring roles began in the first season and persisted until the last: Quark's brother Rom and nephew Nog (Aron Eisenberg), Cardassians Dukat (Marc Alaimo) and Garak (Andrew J. Robinson), Bajoran cleric Adami Winn (Louise Fletcher), the Ferengi Grand Nagus Zek (Wallace Shawn), Chief Miles O'Brien's (Colm Meaney) wife Keiko (Rosalind Chao) and daughter Molly (Hana Hatae/Michelle Krusiec), silent barfly Morn (Mark Allen Shepherd). Behr considered this the series' greatest strength:

> Getting back to telling character-oriented stories, getting back to having conflict between human beings; plot at the service of character. We did our share of space anomalies, usually to screw up O'Brien, [but] I think we created a much more complete universe in which you can have all these characters with all these backstories, all these races, all these supporting characters. You knew more about 'Garak' or 'Gul Dukat', ultimately, than you knew about 'Riker'. So that to me is the contribution.[40]

Sensitive to the zeitgeist of the run-up to the new millennium, *DS9* portrayed conflicts fuelled by religious ideology – and ventured to assert, as no Roddenberry show ever would have, that people other than superstitious dupes might have religious faith. It looked at terrorism as a liberation strategy, the temptations offered by bioweapons, the difficulties of building democratic societies on the ruins of tyranny, and the impulses towards ethnic cleansing and genocide by those engaged in holy wars.

Whereas the starship shows might illustrate such topical issues by visiting a number of different planets or encountering a variety of different species who could allegorise them one at a time, *DS9* weaves them all into an overarching narrative. While never completely serialised like that other 90s' space station show, the 'novel for television' *Babylon 5* (PTEN/TNT 1993–8), it encompasses a seismic historical change from the moment Sisko sets foot on the wrecked station that the Cardassian builders have just abandoned until he and it have weathered a desperate war that almost brings about the subjugation of the entire Alpha Quadrant by the superpower Dominion in response to Sisko's facilitating the creation of a stable wormhole into the Gamma Quadrant where they rule. Not only do the inhabitants of the station accumulate friends, lovers and children, they make decisions and take actions that are crucial in both the initiation and the cessation of this conflict. And some of those decisions and actions derive from their own earlier histories. In no other *Trek* show have the characters' lives prior to the events of the first episode been so central.

Unlike the previous two incarnations of the franchise, *DS9* does not use its characters to represent points on the continuum of emotion and logic, reason and intuition. They are very much individuals, products of their cultures and their histories, both national and personal. All can be passionate or dispassionate, team players or loose cannons, driven by the greater good or ready to sacrifice it for selfish desires. As the Barretts note: 'An acknowledgement of differing agendas and loyalties is central to understanding *DS9*, whether they be ties of family, race, politics, culture or religion, the external factors

Commander
Benjamin Sisko and
Major Kira Nerys

affecting the principal characters have never been so clearly
registered.'[41] This being *Trek*, they will eventually come together as a
cohesive unit working together to achieve a common goal but not before
resolving many conflicts among themselves. The lawman Odo and the
con artist Quark have a bickering, adversaries-who-know-each-other-
better-than-anyone-else rapport reminiscent of Spock and McCoy.
Idealist chatterbox Bashir, the chief medical officer, initially annoys
practical engineer O'Brien, but they go on to become fast friends.
Former Bajoran terrorist Kira Nerys, fiercely resistant to Sisko at first,
comes to admire him immensely.

Despite their carefully delineated differences, parallels exist
among most of the characters. First, they come with a lot of baggage
from their pasts, and concomitant emotional damage. Staff writer
Robert Hewitt Wolfe once referred to the station as 'the island of misfit
toys'. Sisko arrives there psychologically stuck at the moment of his wife
Jennifer's (Felecia M. Bell) death at Wolf 359. Kira grew up under the
brutal Cardassian occupation, lost her parents to it, lived in refugee
camps and killed a lot of people, including civilians, during her time in
the Bajoran resistance. Odo was found floating in space and
experimented upon in a laboratory before revealing his sentience. He
doesn't know who his people are and he too has guilt stemming from the
occupation, when he headed station security under the Cardassians.

O'Brien fought in the war against them and has to deal with his residual prejudices plus his wife Keiko's unhappiness at being taken away from her career as a botanist by his transfer. Bashir was a developmentally delayed child turned into a genius via illegal genetic resequencing. Quark provides reluctant support for his business-failure brother Rom and Rom's son Nog, and never scores the really huge profits that would win him stature in Ferengi society.

The characters battle divided loyalties as well. Kira wonders if she has sold out by working for the Bajoran provisional government and the Federation, and is inevitably stuck in the middle of any disputes between them. The incorporeal, non-linear entities that live within the wormhole, whom the Bajorans worship as 'the Prophets', make Sisko their emissary. He must negotiate the tensions involved with being a religious icon to the Bajorans while serving as a Starfleet officer. Odo eventually discovers his species, the Founders, only to learn that they rule the ruthless Dominion in the Gamma Quadrant. His moral objections to their conduct towards 'solids' constantly war with his deep desire to join them in their communal Great Link. When Worf joins the cast, he brings with him his long and vexed history with his own people and the difficulties his oath to Starfleet have caused in that regard.

Past Prologue

The big story of the battle for the Alpha Quadrant intersects several other narrative strands and sometimes narratives that don't intersect have thematic parallels. The first thread might be called the 'Bajor–Cardassia problem'. The Bajorans are emerging from sixty years of brutal colonialism that has left 15 million dead. A society sustained by profound religious faith, they must restore the infrastructure and economy, unite squabbling factions into a cohesive government and balance the authority of the secular Council of Ministers, headed by the First Minister, with the theocratic Vedek Assembly, headed by the Kai. At the same time, Cardassia is still a near neighbour. On the one hand, the Bajorans keep looking over their shoulders for a renewed Cardassian invasion, since they never would have cut their losses and retreated before the Bajoran Resistance movement if they had known that Bajor and Terok Nor/Deep Space Nine stood at one end of the stable wormhole to the Gamma Quadrant. On the other hand, there are tentative moves towards reconciliation and forgiveness, despite the horrors of the past. Kira, the Bajoran liaison on the station, is the focal point for these stories. She has to learn to trust that the Federation contingent, a necessary evil because Bajor is not strong enough to protect the wormhole on its own, will not simply replace the Cardassians as occupiers. After fighting authority since the age of thirteen, she has to be able to exercise authority, sometimes in ways that remind her of those she had fought against in the Resistance ('Past Prologue', 'Progress'). She gradually learns that not every Cardassian is a genocidal monster, her breakthrough coming in the haunting 'Duet', when the supposed war criminal she engages with in intense interrogation sessions turns out to be a lowly military file clerk, Aamin Marritza (Harris Yulin), who is trying to assuage his guilt for failing to halt atrocities by taking on the identity of his sociopathic superior and seeking public trial and execution at the hands of the wronged Bajoran people. Kira and the Bajor–Cardassia arc come full circle when the

94

Kira confronts
Marritza

Cardassians, having become puppets of the Dominion, rebel and launch the kind of resistance the Bajorans used to fight them – complete with Kira's presence as adviser on how to organise a terrorist insurgency.

The other series-spanning plot arc concerns Sisko's relationship to the aliens who inhabit the wormhole. These incorporeal beings exist simultaneously throughout time; having evolved from a lower species native to Bajor, they feel a connection to the Bajorans and from time to time send them Orbs which reveal prophecies. This makes them the central figures of worship in Bajoran religion, with their habitation within the wormhole dubbed 'the Celestial Temple'. Upon their first encounter, Sisko teaches the wormhole aliens the concept of linear time through the example of the extinct sport he loves, baseball. They then pronounce him their emissary, making him a sacred figure in the eyes of the Bajorans. In the end it is revealed that the Prophets engineered Sisko's birth, since he would be instrumental in saving them from fallen members of their species, the Pah-wraiths.

The emphasis given to these subsidiary plot arcs tracks with the various stages of the overriding opposition between the Dominion and the Federation and its allies. These stages in turn parallel closely changes in *DS9*'s writing staff. In the first two seasons, the Bajor–Cardassia arc dominated, with the Dominion introduced only in vague whispers until their threat to the Alpha Quadrant manifested itself in the season two finale, 'The Jem'Hadar'. Staff writers for these seasons included Piller and Behr, James Crocker, Peter Allan Fields and Robert Hewitt Wolfe. By the start of the third season Piller was concentrating on the launch of *Voyager* and though technically still an executive producer on *DS9* had no writing credits. Fields, who had excelled at writing episodes involving Kira's conflicted relationship with her terrorist past, left the staff, along with Crocker. As Behr assumed show-running duties, he co-wrote most of his teleplays with Wolfe. Joining them were Ron Moore and René Echevarria, fresh from the *TNG* staff.

This staff presided over the first phase of the Dominion's campaign, in which the Founders are revealed to be Odo's shape-shifting

95

people and their primary tactics involve the impersonation of Alpha
Quadrant individuals for the purpose of information-gathering,
infiltration and sabotage, and creating distrust among the various great
powers. The addition of Worf to the cast in season four is accomplished
through a rupture in the Klingon–Federation alliance, as the Klingons
attack a weakened Cardassia and the Federation takes its side. The
beginning of season five reveals that the Klingon aggression had been
fomented by a Founder posing as Chancellor Gowron's (Robert
O'Reilly) chief military adviser, Martok (J. G. Hertzler). By its finale, the
covert phase of the conflict has ended. Dukat, disgraced and turned
renegade when it was revealed that he had a daughter, Tora Ziyal (Cyia
Batten/Tracy Middendorf/Melanie Smith), with his Bajoran mistress
during the occupation, sees his chance to regain power by staging a
military coup against the civilian government, backed by the Dominion,
who send a sizable fleet to base itself in Cardassia. The season-ending
cliffhanger, 'A Call to Arms', shows Starfleet mining the wormhole and
the station being evacuated as Dukat and the Dominion storm in. Sisko
and his staff join an immense Federation fleet ready for the shooting war
that will take up the series' last two seasons. These would be the most
serialised run of episodes: a six-hour start to season six, which deal
with the Federation regaining the station, and the nine hours that
conclude season seven, from the start of the Cardassian rebellion to the
cure offered by Odo to the besieged and dying Female Founder (Salome
Jens), the Dominion leader, and her agreement to cease hostilities.

Wolfe left the staff at the end of season five and Hans Beimler,
who had come on board that year, became Behr's writing partner. It
would be Behr and Beimler who developed the more activist role for the
Prophets; it begins when, challenged by Sisko in 'Sacrifice of Angels' to
do something more for Bajor than sit back and send cryptic messages,
they save the Alpha Quadrant alliance from defeat by making the
Dominion reinforcements disappear as they try to come through
the wormhole.

To connect these disparate plot arcs, the writers provide a
nexus in the rivalry between Sisko and Dukat. Dukat was the last

Dukat vs Sisko

military prefect to preside over the occupation; the Cardassian withdrawal, against his wishes, has branded him a failure. Sisko occupies his old office in Ops, and Dukat's desire to reclaim it is palpable. A self-absorbed egotist with an almost pathological desire to be loved and admired, Dukat is not satisfied with ruling by force. He wants those he subjects to be grateful for the boot on their neck. 'A true victory is to make your enemy see they were wrong to oppose you in the first place, to force them to acknowledge your greatness,' he tells the far more pragmatic Vorta Weyoun (Jeffrey Combs). So the Bajorans' veneration of Sisko as the emissary is another humiliation. Dukat shifts into the Dominion War plot when he becomes the first Alpha Quadrant leader to ally with the Founders. Their support allows him to reclaim command of the station for a time, but when he again loses it, along with Ziyal, who first repudiates his politics and then dies in his arms after being shot as a traitor by his trusted aide Damar (Casey Biggs), he suffers a complete mental breakdown. In this deranged state the grudge he nurses against Sisko mutates into a desire to punish the Prophets as well. Possessed by a Pah-wraith he releases from an ancient artefact, Dukat becomes their emissary. (The resultant glowing red eyes unfortunately take the Pah-wraith plot into cheesy B-movie territory.) He and Kai Winn, who has also envied her people's love for Sisko, combine forces in a scheme to release the Pah-wraiths from the Fire Caves to which the Prophets consigned them. In a final struggle, Sisko throws himself and Dukat off a precipice to prevent this apocalypse and is taken by the Prophets to live with them in the Celestial Temple.

Faith and Treachery

Other parallels help to structure the diffuse seven-year-long narrative of *DS9*. In the more peripatetic starship shows, certain non-Federation behaviours tended to be abstracted from the cultures that indulged in them. One might remember single episodes that warned against abusing telepathic powers or oppressing minority populations – or substituting religious beliefs for rational empiricism – but there was little sense of the total culture of the aliens of the week or of how such transgressive behaviours might vary among different cultures. With the number of cultures receiving detailed attention on *DS9*, this is not a problem. Religion for Roddenberry was always simply a con game run by sometimes very powerful but definitely non-divine life forms who used it to enslave credulous populations and steal their resources. The thinking is far less binaristic here. Not only do the Bajorans worship the Prophets (while extremist cults embrace the Pah-wraiths), but the Dominion's shock troops and front men, the Jem'Hadar and Vorta, consider the Founders to be gods. Even the Ferengi have constructed an elaborate system of theology and ritual based on the worship of profit. The episode 'Treachery, Faith and the Great River' even serves as a sort of comparative religion seminar on the two beliefs. Although no Starfleet personnel other than the special case, Sisko, stray so far from the Roddenberry vision as to become openly devout – Dax constantly reminds Sisko that the Prophets are simply wormhole aliens – the series itself demonstrates where these beliefs come from and how they work for each culture. With their omniscience concerning past, present and future, the 'non-linear' Prophets can send messages about what is to come that are reliable and worth attention. The Founders, through genetic engineering and procreation in labs and hatcheries, really are the creators of the Vorta and Jem'Hadar, so it's hardly a surprise they are worshipped as such. To paraphrase Arthur C. Clarke, any sufficiently advanced alien ability approaches the condition of divinity. The non-theistic Ferengi religion codifies and sanctifies cultural practices that oppress and marginalise certain populations (women and poor businessmen), making it more difficult for them to gain power. Religion becomes dangerous only when species believe that what is culturally appropriate for them is the one true faith, while what is culturally appropriate for others is mere superstition. This is pointed up in dialogue between Damar and Weyoun concerning Dukat's burgeoning obsession with the mysteries of Bajoran religion:

WEYOUN: All this talk of gods strikes me as nothing more than superstitious nonsense.
DAMAR: You believe that the Founders are gods, don't you?
WEYOUN: That's different.
DAMAR: In what way?
WEYOUN: The Founders *are* gods.

Because so much of the *DS9* meta-narrative looks at struggles for power, and particularly at asymmetrical warfare as a method of prevailing in them, these practices also receive consideration in multiple cultural contexts. Resistance/terrorism (depending on one's point of view) recurs with the radical Bajorans, who don't like the Federation any better than the Cardassians; with Cardassian dissenters who want to overthrow military rule; with Kira organising a Resistance to the Dominion occupation of the station; and with the Cardassian uprising against the Dominion. All the major adversaries think nothing of indulging in genocide. The Cardassian occupation of Bajor used forced labour and mass displacement of the indigenous population in order to strip the planet of resources and ready it for eventual colonisation. The Dominion will leave quiescent subject worlds in relative peace but deal ruthlessly with opposition, as seen in the disease loosed on the planet in 'The Quickening'. When the Female Founder has her back against the wall thanks to the defection of the Cardassians, she orders her troops to kill 'all of them'. Before the Federation can stop them, hundreds of millions of Cardassians die, their own genocide coming full circle on them, with compound interest.

In all other *Trek* incarnations the Federation would be moved to indignant protest by such strategies, but in *DS9* the Federation is indulging in them as well. The Maquis terror organisation, introduced here, springs up to combat another Cardassian occupation, this time of the former Federation colonies ceded to them. A good friend of Sisko's, Cal Hudson (Bernie Casey), joins ('The Maquis' (Parts 1 and 2)); Federation security liaison Eddington (Kenneth Marshall) turns out to have been a Maquis mole who tricks his commander out of some industrial replicators headed for Cardassia. Even Sisko's lover Kasidy Yates is a Maquis sympathiser who smuggles supplies for them ('For the Cause'). Of course, there had always been rogue Starfleet officers in *Trek*. More troubling, however, is the revelation that the Federation has since its inception fielded its own covert operations agency, named Section 31 (after the secret clause in the Federation charter which authorised it). One of its sinister operatives, Sloan (William Sadler), tries to recruit the spy-fantasy-loving Bashir into the real thing. Most shocking, though, is the revelation in the series-ending arc that Section 31, with the collusion of the highest ranks of Starfleet Command, has developed a disease that can kill Changelings and have used Odo as a carrier to infect the Great Link. When Odo becomes symptomatic, Bashir and O'Brien kidnap Sloan and learn the cure from him. Odo's offering to link with and cure first the Female Founder and then the rest of the Link ends the war. So while *DS9*'s featured characters repudiate this genocide and forestall it, the

Dominion might have prevailed had the Link not been infected in the first place.

And even the featured characters don't have completely clean hands. 'In the Pale Moonlight' finds Sisko recording a personal log that details his covert attempt to draw the Romulans away from their non-aggression pact with the Dominion to come into the fight on the side of the Federation and its allies. His initial plan isn't wholly dishonourable. He approaches Garak and asks him to see if any of his old spy cronies on Cardassia might dig up evidence that the Dominion will move on the Romulans in time, as Sisko suspects they will. By the time Garak has made some modifications to the plan, however, forged evidence of Dominion duplicity has been authenticated by a Romulan senator's shuttle being blown up, ostensibly by the Dominion but actually by Garak with Sisko's unwitting contrivance. When Sisko angrily calls Garak on what he has done, Garak responds:

Garak plays the devil on Sisko's shoulder

> That's why you came to me, isn't it, Captain, because you knew I could do those things that you weren't capable of doing. Well, it worked and you'll get what you want, a war between the Romulans and the Dominion. You may have just saved the entire Alpha Quadrant . . . and all it cost was the life of one Romulan senator, one criminal and the self-respect of one Starfleet officer. I don't know about you but I'd call that a bargain.

Sisko concludes his log with the reflection that he probably *can* live with what has happened – and then deletes the log.

Earlier in the series Sisko had told his father that 'It's easy to be a saint in paradise.' Behr was deeply sceptical that the utopian future and Starfleet code of ethics presented in *Trek* could survive any serious external threat. Even *TNG* occasionally hinted that this was true: the changed timeline in 'Yesterday's Enterprise' (which Behr co-wrote), the alternate reality in 'Parallels', in which a desperate Riker is willing to destroy the other *Enterprise*s rather than stay where 'the Borg are everywhere'. *DS9*'s Federation does what it must to stave off annihilation, but it forfeits *Trek*'s moral high ground in the process. Perhaps for this reason, Bajor's entrance into the Federation, which seemed to be the series' fitting narrative end point, is still pending as *DS9* concludes.

Identity Crises

The depiction of a Federation both adhering to and departing radically from the template of the Roddenberry vision points to the key area of anxiety in the *DS9* narrative: the impossibility of maintaining a coherent identity or discerning one in others. While this relates to the themes of possession, bodily transformation, duplication and splitting that occur in all the *Trek*s, there is a significant difference. As most of the episodes dealing with those phenomena played out, what was in question was the effacement of one identity by another. The solution was either that the invading identity was purged/reintegrated and the person returned to status quo ante, or the takeover was complete and the original identity erased. Although it too featured episodes that worked like this, the larger issue on *DS9* was that beings 'contain multitudes' inherently. The Barretts point to this anxiety as posing 'the post-modern question of the self: does the individual have a "core" identity that is unshifting?'.[42] This instability is frightening, sometimes for good reason, but also marvellous, and attempts to make others divest themselves of or repress aspects of themselves to allay one's own anxieties are revealed finally as a form of bigotry.

Foregrounding this concern are the Changeling species to which both Odo, in charge of security and justice on the station, and the ruthless Founders belong. Even though he can transform his embodied form into literally anything, his name means 'nothing', a result of a Bajoran mistranslation from the Cardassian of the label 'unknown sample' when he was just a beaker of amber goo in a lab. From the humanoid point of view, Changelings threaten because they can't be pinned down as any one

Odo mentors an infant Changeling

specific entity, while at the same time they can mimic the identities of other animate and inanimate objects, can impersonate and infiltrate at will. Furthermore, they frequently merge their individual selves into a collective, the ocean-like Great Link, where all minds become one. (The Female Founder makes the analogy of individual drops that can exist independent of the ocean but become indistinguishable from it when returned to the sea.) The combination of individuality submerged in a collective and the lack of a stable unique identity represents the primal fears of the *Trek* universe as portrayed in *Star Trek* and *TNG*.

From the moment in 'The Adversary' when a Changeling posing as Starfleet Admiral Krajensky (Lawrence Pressman) is killed while sabotaging the *Defiant* and whispers as his last words, 'You're too late. We're everywhere', the Federation grows increasingly paranoid. Blood screenings become routine. Time and resources are diverted to better ways to locate Changeling infiltrators. Civil rights take a back seat to security. As the two-parter 'Paradise Lost/Homefront', set on Earth, makes clear, for all the damage done by actual infiltrators, the damage done by the fear of them is equally injurious to all the Federation stands for.

But *DS9* gives us the opposite perspective as well. To the Changelings, those life forms that can't change shape are pitied for their limited, locked-in-a-prison-of-flesh existence. Because Odo killed the Krajensky impostor, becoming the first Changeling ever to harm another, the Link sentences him not to death but to what they consider worse than death: life as a solid. The Dominion operates as it does partly because the Founders can view solids as inferior and disposable, but even more so out of a justified fear of persecution. We learn in several episodes of a long history of violence against Changelings by solids, with them only achieving safety when they were able to manufacture their fearsome Jem'Hadar army. An origin myth among the Vorta, which Weyoun relates in 'Treachery, Faith and the Great River', states that the ancestors of the Vorta were proto-hominids who once gave shelter to a wounded and hunted Changeling; the Founders later reciprocated by genetically engineering the Vorta to be their sentient and worshipful servants. (As a variant on Changeling multiplicity, Vorta 'models' are clones. When one dies, another who looks exactly the same and retains all the memories and experiences of the previous incarnations seamlessly takes over.) The Female Founder tells Odo that 'to become a thing is to know a thing'. Given their paranoia, this means for the Founders that mimicking members of a certain species will let them discover vulnerabilities and weaknesses to be used to control them. But the aphorism bespeaks empathy as well. It is this other facet of knowledge gained by imitation that Odo will bring to the Link when he leaves to cure it in the series finale.

Odo is not the only regular character to have multiple bodily identities. As joined Trills, Jadzia and Ezri Dax house the long-lived Dax symbiont, who presumably has a consciousness of its own but also contains all the memories of all the previous host bodies it has inhabited. Each host has to perform a balancing act in which he or she integrates these past incarnations with the individual personality he or she developed before being joined. The previous Dax host, Curzon (Frank Owen Smith), had been a friend and mentor to Sisko, and he continues to call the young female Jadzia 'old man', his affectionate term for Curzon. Dr Julian Bashir has to come to terms with where (or if) the developmentally delayed child his parents call Jules resides in the genetically modified genius they turned him into.

105

Bashir confesses his genetic enhancements to O'Brien

Other more temporary bodily changes or multivalences take place throughout the series. Dukat, who seems to crave the love of the Bajorans more than the approval of his Cardassian compatriots, has himself surgically altered to appear Bajoran as he seduces Kai Winn to help him with his plot to release the Pah-wraiths. In 'Second Skin' Kira awakes after being abducted to find herself looking like a Cardassian and spends the rest of the episode wondering whether or not she is really a deep cover Cardassian agent named Iliana Ghemor who, with her own memories suppressed, has lived Kira's life for the past decade, while the real Kira Nerys is dead. On the level of psychic identity, Sisko not only has to reconcile being the emissary of the Prophets and a Starfleet captain, but to make sense of a vision the Prophets send him that implies he is Benny Russell, an African-American science-fiction writer of the 1950s who has invented the world of *DS9* as an antidote to the racist society he lives in, casting people from his real life in the roles of the characters of his fiction, which in its own time is suppressed because supposedly no American would believe in a black man commanding a space station ('Far Beyond the Stars'). At the conclusion of the episode, Sisko looks out his window and sees Benny Russell reflected back at him, leaving him to ponder whether he is 'the dreamer or the dream'.

These literal examples also stand as metaphors for the constantly evolving psychic spaces all the characters traverse as they face conflicting emotions, changing agendas and renegotiated alliances. These unstable selves are then balanced against intrinsic identities that can't be easily effaced, most frequently those having to do with family and with race. Moreover, even between these more stable identities, intractable conflicts often arise.

Ties of Blood and Nation

To analyse the function of family in *DS9* is impossible without considering the characters' extensive immersion in local politics and how the two are interlinked. Although there are individual episodes that deal with family life in a purely domestic context – the much-praised Sisko–Jake story 'The Visitor', for example – the overall arc the series traverses emphasises the vulnerability of familial relations to political exigencies. In the end, the blood ties that link characters to their own species and homeworld – the *Trek* equivalent of Earth's ethnicity and nationality – frequently supersede the more intimate ties of kinship. Therefore, although *DS9* is far from treating family members as the annoying encumbrances they so often are in the other series, it still hesitates to grant personal domestic lives primacy over the duties individuals owe to the larger family that is their nation. Where *DS9* additionally differs is in its eventual assertion that these ties of nation may take precedence over the supra-national ideology represented by the Federation. To better gauge the balance between the political and the personal that the series advocates for its protagonists, it is instructive to examine the imbalances in that relation as seen in the societies of the Federation's antagonists, the Cardassians and the Founders, and to compare it to the way it works for several other species (Klingon, Ferengi) to which non-Federation principal characters belong.

107

The second season episode 'Cardassians' traces out the ways in which the concept of family is inseparable from the species' political ideology. Investigation into the case of an abandoned Cardassian war orphan who has been adopted by Bajoran parents, and raised to hate all other Cardassians, reveals that the boy, Rugal (Vidal Peterson), has been a pawn in a drawn-out political rivalry between Dukat and his father, Kotan Pa'Dar (Robert Mandan), a prominent member of the civilian government. Dukat blames Pa'Dar's faction for ordering the evacuation of Bajor by the Cardassians. Because the civilian council also ordered the orphans to be left behind, when an attack on Pa'Dar's family's home leaves his mother dead, Dukat abducts Rugal, depositing him in a Bajoran orphanage. Thinking his son also killed, Pa'Dar leaves without him.

Dukat waits eight years for a time to come when his rivalry with Pa'Dar reaches a critical point and then, under a pretence of concern for the abandoned children whose plight is a 'disgrace' to

Cardassia, sets in motion events that will expose Pa'Dar as having left his son behind on Bajor. When Pa'Dar comes to the station to retrieve the boy, he confesses that 'on Cardassia family is everything . . . and I have failed in my responsibility to my family'. The public revelation of this failure is sure to end his career, just as Dukat has planned all along. He hasn't counted on his long-standing enemy Garak, however. Garak and his friend Dr Bashir in turn expose Dukat's machinations. Since each party now has information that would embarrass the other politically, the whole affair will never become public knowledge on Cardassia.

'Cardassians' additionally reveals that family relations do not simply become fodder for political intrigue, but that the very nature of family is defined by the state in ways that negate mere blood ties or natural compassion. Garak reveals that 'children without parents have no status in Cardassian society'. Tellingly, Pa'Dar, despite his own wrenching experience, demurs at using the political clout Sisko has helped him salvage in order to comply with the commander's request that he help bring these stateless orphans home. (Also telling is Sisko's decision that Rugal should be returned to his biological father despite his strong desire to remain with his Bajoran parents. It is the opposite of Picard's decision to let the human boy Jono remain with his alien adopted father in the similarly themed *TNG* episode 'Suddenly Human'.)

Although 'Cardassians' deals only with Garak and Dukat's politics, without reference to their families, in subsequent episodes it becomes clear how both their lives offer near textbook examinations of the conflict that haunts so many Cardassians, a conflict between affection for blood kin and the definition of the family unit as sanctioned by the state. While Dukat's concern for the welfare of the abandoned war orphans is a hypocritical ruse, the parent–child bond is something he values highly. When Sisko reluctantly takes him on as an ally in actions involving the rogue Federation citizens who have formed the Maquis terrorist group, Dukat makes a point of bragging about his seven children and talking to Sisko as one father to another.

Rugal and Pa'Dar

As the fourth season episode 'Indiscretion' reveals, however, the state ideology puts Dukat's paternal feelings to the test. He has believed Ziyal to have been killed when the transport evacuating her and her mother to safety on Liseppia crashed. Six years later, evidence that there may have been survivors surfaces. Kira assumes he is eager to reunite with his daughter and is stunned when he says: 'Not quite. You see, if my daughter is still alive, I have no other choice but to kill her.' He explains that siding with the new civilian government has made his political position tenuous, and that he has 'many enemies that wouldn't hesitate to use Ziyal against me'. He declares that his state-sanctioned duty is only to his wife and his legitimate children: 'They are my family, the one I must protect.' 'You would kill your own daughter to save your career!' Kira protests, and Dukat never satisfactorily refutes this interpretation.

Prevented by Kira's intervention from killing Ziyal immediately, Dukat undergoes a change of heart. He embraces her and takes her back to Cardassia with him, going against the state's narrow definition of family. Through the various ups and downs in his standing within Cardassian society that follow, Dukat's loyalties to his hybrid daughter wax and wane as well. She eventually cannot maintain a daughter's loyalty to him if it means she must choose the Cardassian side in politics, and it is tragic but fitting that she is executed as a traitor by Dukat the politician's most trusted ally, dying in the arms of Dukat the father, who forgives her.

Ziyal's love for her father never overrides her distaste for Cardassian political ideology. Garak, with whom she ironically falls in love, takes the opposite course. Presumably illegitimate as well, he is always kept at arm's length by his father, Enabran Tain (Paul Dooley). Although never acknowledging paternity, even when Garak begs it of him when he is on his deathbed, Tain has long exploited the blood tie that makes Garak such an eager-to-please subordinate, but feels no pangs about sacrificing him to his own political agenda. For Garak, serving the state in the most ruthless fashion is the only way he can have any relationship to his father in blood but not in law, and it's a soul-destroying path he gladly takes. Yet, in doing so, he clearly violates some better part of his nature, as evidenced in his crippling claustrophobia, addiction and other incidents of emotional collapse.

These tragic dimensions of family relationships among the Cardassians point to a critique of states that require citizens to subordinate blood to nation, but it also indicates the strength of blood ties. No matter how ceaselessly the state indoctrinates its citizens about the political function of the family, individual Cardassians again and again respond to the pull of love for children or parents that politics contravenes. Although such defiance frequently causes the state to crush these individuals, its constant resurfacing seems to indicate that ideology can never completely co-opt familial affection. Even to these 'bad guys' blood ties are far more meaningful (and powerful) than they are to the collective crews of the two Federation starships *Enterprise*.

The Cardassians' tragically conflicted interminglings of family and politics stand in sharp relief to what goes on in the society of the series' other major antagonists, the Founders. Because of their radically different physiology from the solid aliens in the Alpha Quadrant, the Founders have been able to collapse the distinction between family and nation. When Odo finally discovers the Changeling homeworld, he eagerly enquires if he might meet any family members. The Female Founder informs him that he already has because 'we are all part of the Great Link' ('The Search' (Part 2)). The merging of individual essences that constitutes linking has overtones of both familial bonding and erotic ecstasy, so that Odo's vexed interactions with the Female Founder always evoke a sinister, quasi-incestuous maternity on her part.

To make sure that the solid functionaries who administer and defend the Dominion never become caught up in any family vs state dynamics, the Founders have done away with any blood ties among them. Artificial species manufactured in laboratories, Jem'Hadar and Vorta have no parents or children. Furthermore, because the Founders recognise the strong pull of blood ties for solids, they exploit it as a weakness, striking at the family structure in order to punish rebellion. In 'The Quickening' the Founders infect everyone on a disobedient subject world with a latent disease that can activate at any time and that is always passed on to offspring. When Damar breaks with the Dominion and urges Cardassia to rise up and throw off the Dominion yoke, the first thing the Female Founder does is to order that his family be found and killed.

Among the solids, the Klingons most fully integrate family into national identity. Organised around a clan system of 'houses' in a warrior society, which resembles those of the feudal eras of human history, Klingon culture treats the actions of any one member of the family as a reflection on the actions of all. Whereas the Cardassian paradigm most frequently involves a familial lapse bringing about political ruin, for Klingons, political defeats bring ruination to family. On *DS9* this principle is illustrated when Worf sides with the Federation against Klingon Chancellor Gowron's war on Cardassia. As revenge, Gowron strips the House of Mogh of all rights and property and eliminates its seat on the Klingon High Council. This loss of honour so discomfits Worf's brother Kurn (Tony Todd) that, in 'Sons of Mogh', he comes to the station in despair, demanding that Worf ritually murder him. When Dax intervenes, there are efforts to integrate the houseless Kurn into the station's society of exiles and misfits, but neither they nor his blood tie to Worf can provide Kurn with a motivation to keep on living. Worf finally resorts to the radical solution of erasing Kurn's memories and creating a new identity for him as a member of the House of Nogra, headed by an old friend of Mogh. Here we see that membership in a Klingon house is a necessity to participate in the culture, but that such membership can be conferred based on ties of friendship as well as kinship. The series reiterates this point as Worf later gains readmission to Klingon society when his comrade in arms, General Martok, invites him to join his house.

Quark's Ferengi clan, the family group featured almost as prominently as the Siskos, hails from a culture where both blood and nation take a back seat to the overriding principle of every-man-for-himself profiteering. This society consigns women to the home, decrees that they stay naked and forbids them to acquire profit, although they can set terms for contracting out their services as sexual partners and bearers of children. We learn that Rom's partner and Nog's mother, Prinadora, swindled Rom out of the money he paid her to extend the contract and left him with the boy. Because of this skewed definition of family, Ferengi who are related by blood do not share (or even have, as far as we know) common surnames. Quark frequently addresses Rom and Nog as 'Brother' and 'Nephew', as if these locutions are necessary to remind them of their kinship.

Quark and Rom's mother, Ishka (Andrea Martin/Cecily Adams), however, is a very clever and forceful woman who begins donning clothes surreptitiously and earning profit. She subsequently becomes the lover of Grand Nagus Zek and ends up running the entire Ferengi economy through him, while at the same time convincing Zek to grant women full political rights and make other democratic reforms. This task completed, she and Zek retire, passing the leadership on to her favoured son, Rom, who is a business failure like his father but an

Quark and his extended family

engineering genius who goes to work for the Federation (as his son Nog joins Starfleet); both serve with distinction during the Dominion war.

While this scenario would seem to paint 'Moogie' as a visionary and feminist role model, it is unfortunate that the domestic tangles in this only family on the series to be headed by a woman are usually played as farce and Ishka is portrayed as a comic harridan somewhat akin to the manner in which *TNG* depicts Lwaxana Troi. *DS9* thus suffers from the same tendency to employ gender stereotypes, especially of the maternal, as do the other *Trek* series. As Ilsa Bick observes:

> The *Enterprise*'s grip on Kirk, however, seems more that of a greedy, smothering mother, with the erotic implications of this surrender split off to other female characters, effectively dividing the maternal into two, disparate images. These good/chaste and bad/sexual mothers and their representatives predominate in *Star Trek*.[43]

The Female Founder and Moogie resonate as ungovernable, domineering, sexually transgressive women, while the good mother, Jennifer Sisko, is also a dead mother. Two-parent families are rare on the series, and the more loving the parent–child relationship, the more likely it is to involve a single *father* and his child. Only the O'Briens defy this stereotype, but they serve as an exception to the paradigms of family life in the *Trek* universe when they arrive on Deep Space Nine and when they leave it.

In the original series episode 'Journey to Babel' Spock's mother Amanda (Jane Wyatt) tells Kirk that her son is 'neither human nor Vulcan, at home only in Starfleet'. The starship shows broaden this definition beyond those torn by a hybrid racial identity. They imply that to be the best a humanoid can be, one must be at home only in Starfleet, one must put blood and nation second to the transnational, meta-familial community that lives inside a tin can flying through space. *DS9* values the ability of such communities to give sentient life forms the big picture, to allow them to transcend parochial thinking and bigotry. But it also views them as a sort of grand educational institution from which one graduates, achieves maturity and embraces family and nationality in this more enlightened way.

The insistence that maturity demands separation from the cocoon of the station comes through strongly in the series finale, 'What You Leave Behind'. Only the youngest of the Starfleet officers remain there (Bashir, Ezri Dax, Nog), as does Jake. All the regulars who have experienced long-term romantic relationships and/or had children move on. (Quark, the perpetual bachelor, represents a case of arrested development.) Yet if commitment to partners and family life is a sign of the maturation necessary to allow a character to stop being one of Bick's 'boys in space', continued devotion to family does not necessarily constitute the final goal of that maturation. Instead, what calls most insistently to the characters at the end of *DS9* is not blood but nation. Let us consider the places to which the characters depart. The O'Briens return to Earth, where Miles will teach at the Academy. Rom and his second wife Leeta go to Ferenginar as he assumes the post of Grand

Nagus. Worf and Martok will dwell on the Klingon homeworld, where Worf serves as Federation ambassador. Garak ends his long exile and returns to Cardassia. Odo joins the Great Link to begin the long process of teaching the Founders to trust and respect solids. The Prophets take Sisko out of linear time to join them in the Celestial Temple. Kira does stay on to command the station, but it is part of Bajor, her native planet. Thus national duties take precedence over loyalty to the Federation or the eclectic community that formed on the station and, in the cases of Sisko and Odo, require indeterminate absence from loved ones.

A product of the 90s, a decade marked by identity politics and ethnic cleansings, *DS9* naturally casts doubts on the utopian assimilationism of the 60s-inspired Roddenberry vision of the first two series. It concludes as a parable of necessary growth through which the childishly destructive local politics of various nations are transformed by individuals whose values have themselves been reshaped by their years as part of the station's multicultural society, which they must, nevertheless, leave behind to go home.

To many Trekkers, *DS9* departed too far from the Roddenberry vision. It 'boldly sat where no one has sat before'. Its serialised storylines and emphasis on relationships resembled soap opera more than space opera. It painted the Federation in a less than positive light and spent four seasons on a war footing. In retrospect, it stands as a brilliant dead end that future instalments in the franchise more or less ignored. By casting a sceptical eye on the utopian foundations of the *Trek* universe, *DS9* serves a function analogous to those of the outsider characters who comment on the vagaries of the human condition. And, while those characters are a welcome and valued part of each series' ensemble, no one ever lets them be the captain.

5 *Star Trek: Voyager*: Time and Again

Yeah, they didn't have that person who kept Rick at bay and would fight for
what he thought the show was. That didn't exist at *Voyager*.[44]

Ron Moore, *TNG* and *DS9* writer-producer, who quit the *Trek* franchise
after a few months on the *Voyager* season six writing staff

If the *Trek* franchise were a play, Act I would conclude with the
resurgence of the original series in aftermarket syndication and Act II
would conclude with the end of *TNG*, the transfer of the *Enterprise-D*
and its crew to the big screen, and the decision to put the fourth series on
a new broadcast network, UPN, rather than in the first-run syndication
market, which was becoming crowded with competing genre series
at the same time that outlets for syndicated programming were
shrinking. Key to a smooth transition to this new model was continuity
between the *TNG* writers and those who moved to *DS9* and to UPN
anchor *Voyager*.

Although *TNG* had relied upon a number of able freelancers
during its run, its best seasons benefited from a stable of staff writers
with complementary talents, allowing the series a wide range of story
types and a healthy balance between 'high concept' science-fiction
premises, in which crises were solved through bursts of technobabble
and hurried tapping of computer touchscreens, and more character-
centred dramas involving personal or ethical crises. Ron Moore and

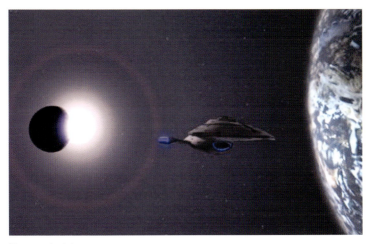

Voyager, lost in space

René Echevarria, the *TNG* staffers who went to *DS9*, fitted in with the more character-centred approach of that show. Moore had been responsible for the exploration of Klingon culture in *TNG*, and when Worf and a Klingon storyline came over to *DS9* the year after Moore did, the match was even more felicitous. Moore preferred warrior characters and military action generally and he had considerable skill in crafting dialogue and portraying moral crises. Echevarria gravitated to softer relationship stories. A master of the moods of loss and longing, he also had an interest in beings who had been studied or experimented on in laboratories, as his later work on *Now and Again* (CBS 1999–2000), *Dark Angel* (FOX 2000–2) and *The 4400* (USA Network 2004–7) would demonstrate. On *DS9*, this led him to specialise in episodes centring on Odo.

117

Michael Piller, only heavily involved in the first two seasons of *DS9*, left the *Trek* franchise after *Voyager*'s first season to create and produce *Legend* (UPN 1995–6). Even though that series earned early cancellation, Piller never worked full time on *Trek* again. Jeri Taylor, who co-created the series with Berman and Piller, ran *Voyager* for its first four seasons. She had shown a knack in her *TNG* scripts for writing fanatics: Nora Satie (Jean Simmons) in 'The Drumhead', Kila Marr (Ellen Geer) in 'Silicon Avatar', Ben Maxwell (Bob Gunton) in 'The Wounded' and Gul Madred (David Warner) in 'Chain of Command'. Perhaps a bit too much of this talent leached into the characterisation of Captain Kathryn Janeway, of whom Taylor was the primary architect. Sometimes reckless and obsessive, with a trademark wagging index finger, Janeway is a stickler for protocol who thinks deeply about the emotional well-being and personal development of those under her command, sometimes to the point of making life choices for them against their wills.

The other two *TNG* writers who served lengthy stints on *Voyager* were the high-concept specialists. Brannon Braga, who took over as show-runner in the fifth season and was with *Voyager* from beginning to end,[45] loved 'high camp weird science',[46] alternate timelines, other dimensions and stuff bubbling up via spatial anomalies from subspace, fluidic space or chaotic space. Joe Menosky, on staff from season three through season six and often Braga's writing partner, frequently examined how personal and cultural pasts impinged upon present actions. With his more humanistic interests, even stories about dinosaurs surviving extinction by migrating to and evolving into sentient humanoids in the Delta Quadrant ('Distant Origin') contained more subtle characterisations than Braga's technobabble-heavy concepts.

The different approaches these *TNG* veterans took on their subsequent gigs reveal themselves in the respective episodes *DS9* and *Voyager* produced in 1996 to commemorate the thirtieth anniversary of *Star Trek*. Self-proclaimed original series geeks Moore and Echevarria wrote the teleplay for 'Trials and Tribble-lations', an elaborate, expensive and affectionate tribute to one of *Star Trek*'s most beloved episodes. The plot has several *DS9* personnel going back in time in pursuit of Arne Darvin (a Klingon spy whose cover was blown by Kirk in 'The Trouble with Tribbles'), to prevent him planting a bomb and killing Kirk in revenge. The producers got the original actor who played Darvin, Charlie Brill, to reprise the role, built careful reconstructions of the original *Enterprise* sets, and used CGI to insert the *DS9* cast into footage from the *Star Trek* episode.

By contrast, the *Voyager* episode 'Flashback', written by Braga, was set not in the television continuity but that of the films, on board Sulu's ship the *Excelsior* at the time of *Star Trek: The Undiscovered Country*. From its generic one-word title, a trademark of all the spinoffs except *DS9*, to its generic *TNG/Voyager* plot of an alien having infiltrated Tuvok's brain at the time of his service on the *Excelsior*, 'Flashback' has no real link to the universe of the original series. Any ship upon which Tuvok had served would have sufficed. Janeway, a spectator to this past action via a mind-meld, does take time to comment on the original series' era with a condescending nostalgia:

> It was a very different time, Mister Kim. Captain Sulu, Captain Kirk, Dr McCoy. Space must have seemed a whole lot bigger back then. . . . It's not surprising they had to bend the rules a little. They were a little slower to invoke the Prime Directive, and a little quicker to pull their phasers. Of course, the whole bunch of them would be booted out of Starfleet today. But I have to admit, I would have loved to ride shotgun at least once with a group of officers like that.

Captain Sisko, on the other hand, makes sure before leaving the *Enterprise* that, like any good fanboy, he gets Captain Kirk's autograph.

Saints in Hell

Voyager premises a Starfleet crew stranded seventy-five years from the Alpha Quadrant by the actions of a powerful, dying alien looking for a way to save the planet of the Ocampa for which he has assumed responsibility. They and the Maquis vessel they have been pursuing are forced to combine crews and seek a way home together. Having stranded her crew because she is unwilling to leave the Ocampan homeworld at the mercy of its enemies, the Kazon, Janeway is haunted

119

by a guilt that only a successful journey home can assuage. She also now commands a starship whose first officer, pilot, chief engineer and chief medical officer have died in the catastrophic transition to the Delta Quadrant. Her new operations officer, Ensign Harry Kim (Garrett Wang), is on his first assignment after graduating from Starfleet Academy; the only surviving medical expert is the ship's Emergency Medical Hologram; her security officer and old friend, the Vulcan Tuvok, was undercover infiltrating the Maquis crew, thus having betrayed their new allies as they betrayed the Federation. Although logic would dictate that she promote some experienced officers from the lower decks to the vacant posts, drama dictates that they be filled by the Maquis: disgraced Academy cadet Tom Paris at the helm; hot-tempered, half-Klingon B'Elanna Torres, another Academy washout, as chief engineer; and former Starfleet officer Chakotay, who resigned his commission after the Federation betrayal of his fellow Native Americans, as second in command.

If *DS9* sought to demonstrate that it's only easy to be a saint in paradise, *Voyager* seeks to prove that it's possible to be a saint in hell. From the pilot episode 'Caretaker' all the way through to the series finale 'Endgame' Janeway insists, in what often seems to be a suicidal mania, that her crew conduct themselves as Starfleet officers (despite the fact that a substantial number of them were Maquis at war with Starfleet) and adhere to the principles set out by Starfleet and the Federation, even though they are all alone and faraway from support by or communication with those organisations. What makes the situation even more dire is that the Delta Quadrant's inhabitants seem far more likely to be hostile than random chance would indicate. Many species are quick to warn *Voyager* not to violate their territory, those that appear to have peaceful and welcoming societies frequently reveal a duplicitous and dark side, even aliens in distress whom the crew rescues often bite the hand that feeds them. As Janeway sums up the place in 'Alliances':

> Although some of the species we've encountered here have been peaceful, others seem governed only by their own self-interests. This appears to be a

An apparently
hospitable planet
has a hidden
agenda

region of space that doesn't have many rules. But I believe we can learn
something from the events that have unfolded. In a part of space where
there are few rules, it's more important than ever that we hold fast to our
own. In a region where shifting allegiances are commonplace we have to
have something stable to rely on. And we do. The principles and ideals of
the Federation. As far as I'm concerned, those are the best allies we could
have.

This is one of a number of episodes in which Janeway appears to be
overly rigid in sticking to those principles and ideals, risking the welfare
of the crew or declining an opportunity that might get them home. At
least some of the crew think her reasoning is faulty and either attempt to
convince her to bend the rules or go behind her back and bend them on
their own. Inevitably, Janeway's apparently irrational by-the-book
decision is vindicated.

    At the end of one such episode, 'Prime Factors', Janeway gives
Tuvok the kind of 'more in sorrow than in anger' dressing down that
typifies her reactions to errant crew members:

You are one of my most valued officers and you are my friend. It is vital that
you understand me here. I need you, but I also need to know that I can
count on you. You are my counsel, the one I turn to when I need my moral

121

compass checked. We have forged this relationship for years and I depend on it. I realise you made a sacrifice for me but it's not one I would have allowed you to make. You can use logic to justify almost anything. That's its power, and its flaw. From now on, bring your logic to me. Don't act on it behind my back.

The reason for Tuvok's action is crucial to the way *Voyager* works: 'It is quite simple, Captain. You have made it clear on many occasions that your highest goal for the crew is to get them home. But in this instance, your standards would not allow you to violate Sikaran law. Someone had to spare you the ethical dilemma.'

Not only were *Voyager* audiences expected to believe that Janeway and her crew would cling to Starfleet protocols in their very desperate circumstances, but they were expected to believe that Janeway would continue to operate in this manner when it was what stranded them in the Delta Quadrant in the first place. This becomes even harder to swallow on the several occasions when we are shown Janeway anguished at having made the decision that put the lives of the Ocampans ahead of the well-being of her crew, because it was the principled thing to do. In 'Night', for instance, the guilt puts her into a depressive state so that she won't even come out of her quarters. The paradox doesn't resolve itself until 'Endgame', when it is played out literally between two Janeways.

What had happened on the show between 'Night' and 'Endgame' allows for this resolution. 'Night' kicks off season five, the time of the changing of the guard on the writing staff. Taylor and another female staff writer, Lisa Klink, departed, and Brannon Braga became show-runner of a staff that would be all male from then on out. There had clearly been a plan to make *Voyager* more appealing to men since the introduction in the previous season of 'Borg babe' Seven of Nine, a concept authored by Berman and Braga; the addition of the 'souped up' shuttle designed by Tom Paris, the Delta Flyer, was a move in that direction as well. Janeway stopped role-playing a governess in a Victorian Gothic holo-novel and took to hanging out with holo-Leonardo Da Vinci

Seven of Nine

instead. This is not to say that woman-based stories disappeared. Indeed, the journey to self-discovery of Seven and the burgeoning Tom–B'Elanna romance arguably emphasised the female characters more. Seven also gives Janeway someone to play other than the determined commander who see-saws between Captain America and Captain Queeg. Now she becomes the fierce maternal force, trying to reclaim a lost daughter from the dark side, which came to be personified by the Borg Queen (Alice Krige/Susanna Thompson), a character introduced to Trekkers in the most successful of the *Next Generation* films, *First Contact*, at roughly the same time as Seven joined the cast of *Voyager*.

123

What changed was the fundamental situation. Under Taylor's direction, *Voyager* was about perseverance and survival, but not about victory. Seven's Borg technology and extensive knowledge of every species they ever assimilated give the crew an advantage, and they are far less desperate and vulnerable than in early seasons. Janeway even acquires some Picardian diplomatic savvy and manages to establish trust between the Federation and Species 8472, to help a visionary Hirogen channel his brutal species' hunting instincts into more productive activities, and to persuade the Darwinianly competitive crews trapped within 'The Void' to form a sort of mini-Federation and effect an escape for all.

This is the Kathryn Janeway we meet in 'Endgame', which begins thirty-three years after *Voyager* was stranded in the Delta Quadrant. Janeway, now an admiral, got the ship home ten years before, and a number of the crew have established productive lives back in the Alpha Quadrant. But she is haunted by those she never got home, especially Seven of Nine, whose death shortened in turn the life of her mourning husband Chakotay. (A totally unconvincing Chakotay/Seven romance was cooked up in the seventh season.) It was also too late to reverse a neurological disease that has left Tuvok confined to a mental hospital. Facing a lonely old age with her three closest friends from the voyage gone, the admiral has brooded for some time on one of the many missed opportunities to get the ship home sooner. During the seventh year out they had come upon one of the transwarp hubs the Borg use to travel throughout the galaxy in search of new populations to assimilate. At the time, there was no way *Voyager* could have survived an attempt to use the hub for its own repatriation. Now, however, technology exists that might ensure success and save Seven, Chakotay, Tuvok and twenty-two other crew members. So Janeway violates the Temporal Prime Directive and numerous other Starfleet regulations to take it back to her former self.

In typical Janeway fashion, the captain instead insists that they use the technology to destroy the hub and save millions of future Borg victims, even though the delay will have the consequences the admiral reports. This is, of course, a precise repeat of her decision in the pilot to destroy the array to save the Ocampans. The admiral proceeds to raise every objection to such self-destructive do-gooding that has ever been raised throughout the series. And since she's talking to a version of herself, and one she outranks, she can speak with full candour:

> JANEWAY: I want to know why you didn't tell me about this.
> ADMIRAL: Because I remember how stubborn and self-righteous I used to be. I figured you might try to do something stupid.
> JANEWAY: We have an opportunity to deal a crippling blow to the Borg. It could save millions of lives.

Admiral Janeway squares off against Captain Janeway

ADMIRAL: I didn't spend the last ten years looking for a way to get this crew home earlier so you could throw it all away on some intergalactic goodwill mission.

. . .

JANEWAY: I refuse to believe I'll ever become as cynical as you.

ADMIRAL: Am I the only one experiencing déjà vu here?

JANEWAY: What are you talking about?

ADMIRAL: Seven years ago you had the chance to use the Caretaker's array to get *Voyager* home. Instead you destroyed it.

JANEWAY: I did what I knew was right.

ADMIRAL: You chose to put the lives of strangers ahead of the lives of your crew. You can't make the same mistake again.

The crew as usual come through on the captain's side. Even those with grim futures forecast willingly sacrifice themselves for the greater good, and Harry Kim toasts their journey together as more important in the long run than the return home. Even the admiral sees the light: 'I'd been so determined to get this crew home for so many years that I think I forgot how much they loved being together, and how loyal they were to you. It's taken me a few days to realise it. This is your ship, your crew, not mine.'

Rick Berman says on the season seven DVD special features that for a month in the breaking of the script, the producers had decided to go with this ending and have the ship not get home during the present time of the series.[47] Obviously, they realised that this strategy risked an audience uprising, so once the admiral has said her *mea culpa*, the captain replies: 'There's got to be a way to have our cake and eat it too.' Putting their two heads together, the Janeways contrive a plan for *Voyager* to escape inside a Borg sphere ahead of the shockwave of the exploding hub, albeit at the price of Admiral Janeway's life.

Displacements and Disavowals

Having one's cake and eating it too is a good way to describe how the series deals with an overall premise at war with both the stories it wanted to tell to sustain a seven-year run and with common sense. Once the rebellious Maquis emerge at the end of 'Caretaker' sporting crisp new Starfleet uniforms and answering to Starfleet ranks, viewers know that anything approaching realism has been tossed out of an airlock. It is clear that the producers wanted *TNG* viewers to feel comfortable with this new starship crew and their shiny, clean ship with tastefully decorated rooms. A real vessel in this predicament would soon show jury-rigged systems, frayed uniforms, hull breaches patched to look like a Vidian's face; would experience periodic shortages of raw materials despite the trading missions frequently mentioned; would not have an inexhaustible supply of shuttles to crash and explode; and would not allow the crew the luxury to loll about in power-consuming holodeck simulations of French bistros, nineteenth-century English romance novels and Polynesian resorts. Nor would the captain make frequent detours to examine interesting astronomical phenomena because being lost and alone shouldn't mean that a vessel forgets Starfleet's number one priority to be explorers.

The writers did acknowledge in various ways that the scenario they were offering would not have been very likely to occur. In the third season episode 'Worst Case Scenario' the crew discover a holodeck simulation Tuvok began working on, to prepare for a possible uprising of the crew against the Janeway regime that never came. Its leader, holo-Chakotay, proclaims:

> Under my command, we won't let almighty Federation principles get in the way of opportunities the way Janeway did when she destroyed the array that could have gotten us home. And we won't be wasting precious time stopping to investigate every insignificant anomaly that we come across. What we will do is use any means necessary to acquire technology that can shorten our journey. To hell with Starfleet regulations.

Other episodes mention additional options many ships in *Voyager*'s situation might explore, just so we can see them rejected. In 'The 37s' the crew come across a planet colonised by humans abducted by aliens in the twentieth century and brought to the Delta Quadrant as slaves. Having revolted and driven away their masters, they grow to a vibrant, advanced colony of a hundred thousand strong. They invite any *Voyager* crew who would rather make a new life than pursue the perilous and lengthy journey home to join them. In a rare case of her not trying to decide what's best for her people on her own, Janeway gives them a choice. Of course, the show could not continue if a substantial crew complement defected, but realistically we might see a dozen or so 'redshirts' decide to leave. To make sure that we realise just how committed to their captain they are, however, not a single soul chooses to stay behind. 'Elogium' brings up the issue of coupling and bearing children, of the necessary precaution of breeding replacements should the journey home take the full seventy-five years. The discussion between Janeway and Chakotay is inconclusive, but the episode ends with Ensign Samantha Wildman (Nancy Hower) announcing that she is pregnant by the husband she left behind. Although Naomi Wildman (Scarlett Pomers/Vanessa Branch) subsequently thrives in the shipboard

127

environment, we never see a child conceived on *Voyager* until Paris and Torres's daughter is born in the final minutes of the series finale.

Another tactic involves episodes in which *Voyager* surrogates are set up as straw men to show the danger of ditching Federation protocols in favour of self-interest. This is no more apparent than in '*Equinox*'. The title is the name of another Federation ship, a planetary research vessel, which the Caretaker also whooshed away to the Delta Quadrant. Their first encounter with a hostile species cost them half the crew, and the captain, Ransom (John Savage), admits to Janeway: 'After a couple of years, we started to forget that we were explorers, and there were times when we nearly forgot that we were human beings.' Needless to say, Starfleet protocols are pretty much toast, first indicated when Ransom and his first officer, Burke (Titus Welliver), address each other by their first names. We soon find out the depths to which such apparently harmless lapses can lead. The *Equinox* scientists have discovered that a certain nucleogenic life form can be converted into a fuel that allows the ship to travel at very high speeds. Others of that race come to attack both ships and the *Equinox* crew leave *Voyager* stranded, create an evil version of the EMH and torture Seven for information. We can see that this rogue behaviour is infectious when Janeway appears ready to let the vengeful life forms kill an *Equinox* officer who won't tell her what she needs to know. At the last moment Ransom comes to his senses and tries to cooperate with Janeway; he manages to transport the surviving *Equinox* personnel and the Doctor and Seven back to *Voyager*, sacrificing himself as the *Equinox* explodes. Janeway deprives all the *Equinox* crew of rank and gives them a stern dressing down; they are never seen again, although supposedly remain on *Voyager*.

Mortal Coil

The one likely scenario that *Voyager* has to disavow most insistently is not giving up or going bad but the death of all hands on the trip home.

Unlike the other possibilities, however, this is not simply an inconvenience brought about by the premise. In a symbolic way, coming back from the dead is what *Voyager* is all about; it *is* the premise. Running during the twenty-ninth through the thirty-sixth years of the *Trek* franchise, the series finds the original *Trek* audience and all three of its creators (born between 1945 and 1948) entering middle age and sensing those first inklings of mortality. *Voyager* confronts the inevitability of death and ponders the possibilities of an afterlife, but it also tells stories that compel death to retreat and come looking for us another day. After all, from the point of view of those they left behind in the Alpha Quadrant, everyone on *Voyager* and the Maquis ship died. We hear of a memorial service in the alternate reality of 'Non-Sequitur'. When contact with Starfleet is finally re-established in 'Message in a Bottle', it is like a miraculous resurrection.

Earlier in the series the emphasis is on the risks of trying to prolong life by 'unnatural' means. The dying Caretaker doesn't try to evade his own death, but he does want to replace himself as guardian to the Ocampa and is willing to engage in mass kidnappings and usually fatal medical experiments to identify someone who can assume his specific function. That the Ocampa themselves live very short lives and never focus on lengthening them serves as an antidote to his obsession. The Vidians refuse to succumb to the Phage, which would render them extinct, but the cost of their survival is the lives of all those from whom they harvest body parts or use as lab rats. Their hideous, patched-together bodies resemble those of zombies or decomposing corpses. In 'Warlord' the crew encounters Tieran (Leigh J. McCloskey), a great military leader of the Ilari, who later grew paranoid and tyrannical. Overthrown by a rival faction 200 years before, he was killed and yet his consciousness persists: 'During his reign he became obsessed with his own mortality. He spent most of his time, and Ilari's resources, searching for ways to overcome death. Somehow he's discovered a way to transfer his own mind into someone else's body.' The cruel and duplicitous form his consciousness retains shows that its continuation is perverse.

129

These cautions against trying to hang onto life too long are matched by warnings against undervaluing the world of the living because of the expectation of a better existence after death. Four episodes, 'Emanations', 'Mortal Coil', 'Coda' and 'Barge of the Dead', deal with cultural expectations of what the afterlife will be, confronted with varying degrees of confirmation or refutation. This variety of endings provides the writers with some wiggle room as to the question of whether there is life after death, but all of them point to the fact that it can never be as uncomplicated (or anthropomorphically comforting) as most religious traditions would have it. Living the life one has now is the only certainty.

The Reset Button

Nevertheless the programme shows an absolute compulsion to rehearse the deaths of the central characters, only to cancel them out via one of the science-fiction *dei ex machina* available to the writers. This happened so often that fans coined the term 'pushing the reset button' to describe this storytelling choice. 'Course: Oblivion' starts out as a 'plague' episode in which crew members suffer acute cellular degeneration, their bodies breaking down at the molecular level. When Torres dies, however, her autopsy reveals that this is not the real *Voyager* crew we are seeing. The season before, in 'Demon', the crew had explored a planet rich in a biomimetic compound called silver blood. When it came into contact with humans, it perfectly mimicked both their physical bodies and their minds and memories, becoming sentient for the first time. In a very un-*Trek*-like move, Janeway allowed all the crew and the ship to be so duplicated, so the life forms could create their own community. It had to be too good to last, of course, given the franchise's aversion to duplicates. The process of imitation is so complete that the beings completely forget their origins and believe themselves to be the *Voyager* crew, with the imperative to return to the Alpha Quadrant. Even with this revelation, their Janeway, with a stubbornness that has to be in the way of parody, insists that she can't abandon this goal any more than her

The duplicate crew of 'Course: Oblivion' celebrate Tom and B'Elanna's wedding

original would. But the only possible way to head off total disintegration is to return to the demon planet, a course of action she is convinced of too late. The episode is incredibly poignant as we watch these avatars of the characters we know persevere even though they and the ship are literally falling apart. Just as they come into view of the real *Voyager*, which hears their desperate distress signal, they explode. Their heroic, doomed journey ends without anyone to remember it.

Although other scenarios enact the crew's death through holographic simulations or hallucinations, the reset button is most often pushed in connection with time travel or temporal anomalies. There is even a fifth season episode, 'Relativity', that pokes fun at the overuse of the trope by showing the toll taken on twenty-ninth-century Federation 'time cops' who repeatedly have to clean up the damage done to the timeline by the *Voyager* crew's many temporal incursions. The Barretts conclude that in *Trek*, 'the element of time travel is introduced to underscore and emphasize a proposed or wished-for stability of the human subject across time. *Voyager*'s time travel narratives are particularly focused on the integrity of the human experience.'[48] Philosophy aside, such incursions do also provide the perfect way for the characters to die for real, not through surrogates, but to spring back to life. As in 'Endgame', it's the ideal formula for having one's cake and eating it too. In 'Before and After' Ocampa Kes (Jennifer Lien) is on her deathbed in her ninth year when she suddenly starts moving backward through time. The phenomenon is being caused by chronoton particles from a time-travelling vessel and, just before she vanishes at the point of conception, a future medical procedure stabilises her conveniently at the point where the show's present narrative is occurring.

A far more gruelling ordeal awaits the crew in the two-part 'Year of Hell'. Here the ship is caught in Krenim space for a year while one of the Krenim scientists, Annorax (Kurtwood Smith), who exists outside normal time, uses his ship's chronoton weapons to wipe out whole populations in repeated attempts to reinstate the Krenim Imperium, defeated by its enemies, the Zahl, and at the same time restore the colony where his wife died as the result of one of his earlier interventions in the timeline. It's clear that he will never account for every butterfly effect, but he is beyond reason in his obsession. Over the year of hell, *Voyager* for once looks ravaged and desperate. Many die, Tuvok is blinded and Janeway has all but a skeleton crew leave on the escape pods, because there is insufficient functional space left to support them all. Finally, the captain musters some allies against Annorax's ship, and the last act of the battle has Janeway, alone on *Voyager*, ramming the temporal warship and destroying it and herself in the process. She has a gut feeling, unsupported by any science advanced during the episodes, that if the ship is destroyed, all its temporal meddling will be undone. And it is. *Voyager* again approaches Krenim space, with the Imperium still battling the Zahl, and is warned off from the war zone, a warning she heeds. Meanwhile, Annorax is at home with his wife, who prevails upon him to take a walk with her, leaving the deadly equations unfinished on his desk, at least for long enough for *Voyager* to clear the area.

'Year of Hell' makes a strong case for leaving even destructive timelines alone rather than trying to alter them. What the show condemns in Annorax, however, it sanctions when the lives of series regulars are at stake. 'Timeless', a dry run for 'Endgame', posits that an attempt by the crew to construct a quantum slipstream drive, in order to shorten the journey home, results in a failure that crashes the ship on an ice planet, killing all aboard. Only Chakotay and Harry Kim, riding point in a shuttle so as to radio back course corrections, survive and arrive in the Alpha Quadrant. Haunted by guilt because he feels his calculations were in error and caused the catastrophe, Harry fifteen years later defies Starfleet and devises a method to communicate across time with *Voyager* before the slipstream conduit collapses; although he doesn't get them to the Alpha Quadrant, he changes the timeline so that they remain safe in the Delta Quadrant. Any changes for good or ill that occur in the fifteen years he and Chakotay have been home are discounted, even by Chakotay's lover of many years, who gladly helps in the endeavour. Admiral Janeway's similar actions in 'Endgame' are even more questionable. She inhabits a timeline in which the ship did get home, albeit with losses, and the ten-year reunion that opens the episode reveals many positive outcomes for those who returned. Her actions throw their destinies into question. One cannot help but conclude that she is motivated to alter the timeline only because the three people

133

whom she was closest to – Seven, Chakotay and Tuvok – had bad outcomes and she's been lonely. Certainly none of the previous *Trek* captains would have indulged in such selfish actions. As Jan Johnson-Smith remarks: 'Both "Timeless" and "Endgame" are superficially about individual matters of conscience or desire, but both actions wipe out decades of history for billions of other beings.'[49] 'Endgame' illustrates both the extreme difficulties the writers had in creating a sympathetic persona for Janeway and *Voyager*'s lack of commitment to anything except keeping the franchise going. As Ron Moore observes:

> It's not about anything. It feels to me that it is a very content-free show. It's not really speaking to the audience on any real level anymore. What's happening is that it's very superficial. It talks a good game. It talks about how it's about deep social problems, and how it's about sociological issues, and that it's very relevant. It's about exploration, and it's about the unknown, and all these cute catch phrases, but scratch the surface of that and there is really not much underneath it all. VOYAGER doesn't really believe in anything. The show doesn't have a point of view that I can discern. It doesn't have anything really to say. I truly believe it simply is just wandering around the galaxy. It doesn't even really believe in its own central premise, which is to me its greatest flaw.[50]

The repeated rehearsals of disaster show a writing staff yearning to explore the grittier and edgier territory of 90s' science-fiction television. The repeated resets show the timidity about altering the status quo that was making the franchise increasingly irrelevant as it entered the twenty-first century. Chris Gregory concludes that *Voyager*,

> has often suffered from a lack of overall direction and a general confusion of purpose. . . . While the hard-edged realism and ironic comedy of *DS9* seems to fit perfectly with today's self-consciously postmodern era, the 'new romanticism' of *Voyager* – like the ship itself – appears to be rather out of place.[51]

6 *Enterprise*: Dead Stop

> When people prove that they can write this show, we embrace 'em, we pay
> 'em a lot of money, and we put 'em on staff. Because they're so hard to
> find.
>
> Rick Berman[52]

When Berman and Braga created *Enterprise*, there were quite a few
people out there who had proven that they could write *Trek*. In addition
to those who had cut their teeth under Piller's tutelage on *TNG* and
gone on to write for *DS9* or *Voyager*, there were writers who had done
multiseason stints on the latter two series: Robert Hewitt Wolfe,
Kenneth Biller, Hans Beimler, Bryan Fuller and Michael Taylor. Yet none
of them signed on to *Enterprise*. (By the end of the first season Mike
Sussman, a seventh season *Voyager* staff writer, and Andre Bormanis,
the science consultant who had done freelance scripts for *Voyager*, had
joined the staff.) When Berman was developing those two shows, he
worked with people like Piller and Jeri Taylor, who had lots of
experience with other television universes. Berman and Braga, on the
other hand, had no experience with any dramatic television franchise
other than *Trek*. Moreover, each was strong as a 'concept' man, more
comfortable with plots than characters. This may be why the strength of
every other *Trek* show, its diverse ensemble, was a primary weakness
with *Enterprise*.

   The need to bring in new staff writers might at least have given
the series new perspectives and paved the way for the radically different

Enterprise NX-01

approach that was implied for a series that is not 'your father's *Star Trek*', as Braga proclaimed. Unfortunately, the new voices didn't have the opportunity to make much of a mark on *Enterprise*; during the first season, Berman and Braga had teleplay or story credits on the first seven episodes and wrote stories and/or teleplays for eighteen of twenty-six season one *Enterprise* episodes. Since Berman had never before shouldered that much of the writing load – he had only two previous teleplay credits other than the pilots for *DS9* and *Voyager* – the fifth series soon showed the results of this myopia combined with creative exhaustion.

The aim seemed to be a reboot to draw in a new cohort of younger fans who would not have been around for the original broadcasts of *Star Trek* or *TNG*. The producers, in fact, removed 'Star Trek' from the title, simply calling the show *Enterprise*, and revamped the format for the title sequence and opening credits. One of the reasons the creators gave for doing a prequel was to 'get back to exploration'. In other words, they wanted the ship to go about the discovery of strange new worlds. A difficulty inherent in that aim was that, after three series set in the Alpha Quadrant, longtime viewers were not going to find very interesting any planet or species that didn't turn out to be a major player in the later shows. Perhaps the desired new viewers wouldn't care, but writing off the dedicated *Trek* fanbase was a major risk. Moreover, Berman and Braga repeated the mistake that had plagued *Voyager*. Even though the NX-01 was in contact with Starfleet and could be sent on specific missions, its mandate for the first two seasons was simply to wander through deep space looking for things that were interesting; the effect was often a certain aimlessness, as if the ship were a tour bus rather than the pride of Earth's space navy.

The pilot episode, 'Broken Bow', introduced still another premise to *Enterprise* that complicated its status as prequel and not, as the rest of the show would demonstrate, for the better. Humans get pulled into a conflict involving a Klingon courier wounded in Oklahoma while fleeing pursuit by genetically enhanced members of a species called the Suliban. Their leader, Silik (John Fleck), takes orders from a fuzzy humanoid figure, dubbed 'Mr Future Guy' by fans, who contacts him in a special chamber that links, we soon learn, to the future. In the eleventh episode, 'Cold Front', a human named Daniels (Matt Winston) announces that he is a Starfleet officer from the thirty-first century. By this time, many species have learned how to master time travel, and a 'Temporal Cold War' is going on in several centuries as one group or another tries to change history for its benefit and the others seek to block the changes. The Suliban are fighting as proxies for an anti-Federation faction who seemingly want to prevent Archer from getting the Federation off the ground.

137

Although it never ended up being used this way, the Temporal Cold War also gave the prequel the option to depart from previously established continuity, since another history-changing adventure was always possible down the line to restore it. However, a universe in which history could be changed over and over again would be terrifyingly unstable, like the situation Worf finds himself in as he jumps from one quantum reality to the other in the Braga-scripted *TNG* episode

The Suliban Silik

'Parallels'. It's not a universe in which a crew can feel safe to look for gas giants and meet new aliens without living in a state of existential angst that all their experiences could be cancelled out at any second.

Nothing New Under the Stars

By 2001 both longtime *Trek* devotees and those looking for an introduction to the universe had at their constant disposal DVD sets of the previous series, plus their omnipresence in syndicated reruns. *Enterprise* needed to be distinctive to capture and hold even a Trekker's attention. The move to make the characters more similar to a contemporary viewer by doing a prequel was the dominant strategy. More than those of any of the other starships, the NX-01's interior looks like that of a naval vessel, gunmetal grey, with ladders instead of Jeffries tubes. The uniforms resemble twenty-first-century jumpsuits and the English spoken is more colloquial, if somewhat adolescent, 'son of a bitch' and 'kick you on your ass' being two frequent expostulations. Yet being only 150 years ahead of the audience is still not being contemporary with the audience. *Stargate SG-1*'s (Showtime/Sci Fi 1997–2007) team works for the US Air Force from 1997–2007; Jonathan Archer works for a united twenty-second-century Earth Starfleet on a planet that has abolished most social ills.

And there are hazards to making a prequel. As Lincoln Geraghty observes:

> The utopianism of *Star Trek*'s future is still present but in a rather conservative and backward-looking form. . . . a predestined confidence will help us achieve utopia. As a result, the vast future history of the *Star Trek* universe diminishes as all of humanity's accomplishments and desires are confined within the exceptional rhetoric of a mythical American history. *Enterprise*'s narrative can go no further than its forebears and likewise its prognosis for the future is foreshortened.[53]

139

In the majority of episodes in its first two seasons and a substantial number thereafter, *Enterprise*'s new frontiers for the crew inevitably are well-worn paths for veteran *Trek* viewers. To be sure, on occasion the paths are negotiated quite smartly. 'Observer Effect' combines the situations of aliens taking over crew members' bodies and their using humans as lab rats. 'Twilight' reveals a dark future reset by some handy technobabble, as well as having Archer suffer the cognitive impairment of the protagonist of millennial cult film favourite *Memento* (2000). 'Similitude' again tells the story of a doomed duplicate of one of the regulars. 'Dead Stop' posits an automated starship repair station that derives its power from the humanoid bodies it seizes as payment for its services, a prefiguring of how, in another quadrant, the Borg collective might have sprung into being. 'Doctor's Orders' has Phlox (John Billingsley) replaying Seven's role in 'One' as the sole crew member able to survive out of stasis in an area of space that induces hallucinations.

Of course, the future was not completely closed off to Archer and his crew. The Temporal Cold War could whisk him off there, but its Federation agent, Daniels, only did that once, with disastrous results. Through the first two seasons, the whole conceit remained fuzzy, appearing in only five episodes, with little known about it except that the extremist Suliban, known as the Cabal, and their mysterious sponsors wanted to scuttle Archer's mission. By the end of that second season the failure of *Enterprise*'s narrative formula to retain 50 per cent of its initial audience was apparent and a matter of very public discussion. Disgruntled fans vented their feelings on the internet, even including actress Jolene Blalock, a lifelong Trekker, who played T'Pol. Blalock said she 'was dismayed by early "Enterprise" scripts that seemed to ignore basic tenets of the franchise's chronology, and that offered revealing costumes instead of character development. "The audience isn't stupid." '[54] *TV Guide* solicited input from viewers about 'How to Fix Trek', and for its own part advised 'Make it Ominous'; 'Make it More Real'; 'Open Fire and Close Those Pie Holes'; and 'Get Us on the Edge of Our Seats'.[55]

Berman and Braga would take that advice two months later when the season-ending cliffhanger 'The Expanse' featured an alien

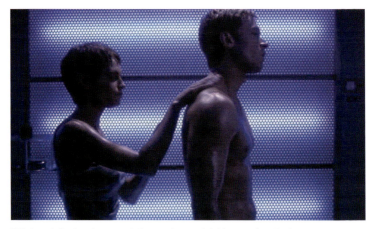

T'Pol and Tucker in one of the controversial 'decon chamber' scenes

Chief Engineer Trip Tucker and Captain Jonathan Archer

attack on Earth that kills 7 million people, including Trip Tucker's sister. Archer learns from Silik and his future sponsor that this was a dry run and the offending aliens, the Xindi, plan to return with a more powerful weapon to destroy Earth in a pre-emptive strike, because they believe that Earth will, in the future, destroy them. *Enterprise*'s entire third season would deal with the newly up-armoured NX-01, its crew supplemented by a combat detachment called MACOs, navigating a treacherous and unstable area of space called the Delphic Expanse in a desperate quest to stop the deployment of the Xindi planet killer.

141

This scenario lined up much more with those of contemporary twenty-first-century space-based series like *Stargate SG-1* and *Farscape* in which Earth's very existence hangs in the balance of the crew's fight against the 'big bads'. It also returns to the immediate post-9/11 universe of *Enterprise*'s debut, a time when the Suliban (named for the Taliban) could easily be seen as radical Islam and Archer's American human chauvinism, his mixture of resentment, arrogance and cluelessness, could be read as mimicking George W. Bush's desire to go it alone and reject the cautious multilateralism recommended by the Vulcan High Command (read: 'Old Europe').

But the writers made several crucial mistakes in executing this plot arc (not least in having the Xindi tip their hand via the dry run rather than testing the prototype on some Earth-like planet and using the element of surprise to obliterate humankind when the killer weapon was ready). Although the strange properties of the Expanse are eventually explained as the attempt by the Sphere Builders, aliens from another dimension, to transform that space into a region hospitable for their colonisation, it set the stage for the reflexive 'spatial anomaly' storylines that previous series had overused. And with the chance to focus the Temporal Cold War and let it carry a sustained storyline, the writers instead muddied the waters unnecessarily. Having established the Suliban Cabal as the chief adversary for two years, what would have been more logical than to have it developing the weapon within the Expanse at the behest of Mr Future Guy, who turned out to represent the Sphere Builders? The portrayal of the Xindi nation as multispecies, with sentient beings having evolved into humanoids, sloths, insectoids, reptilians and aquatics, is a welcome change from *Trek*'s tendency to treat alien worlds as having a single race and culture, down to lock-step clothing and hairstyles. But that would have been a better concept to explore in subsequent narrative arcs, rather than abruptly shifting focus away from the Suliban Cabal. Even the twist that had Archer convince Degra (Randy Oglesby), the Xindi-humanoid designer of the weapon, that he and his planet are being manipulated could work with a Suliban, whose population had previously been shown to have various ideological positions *vis-à-vis* the actions of the most radical elements. By bringing in a completely unfamiliar alien species, the writers were asking the audience for a new investment of their attentions rather than paying off one already in place.

Back to Basics

Ratings improved marginally for the third season, but it's doubtful that a better execution of the Xindi season would have made much difference, since no more than 4.5 million viewers ever tuned in to sample it. The network, now part of a larger media conglomerate produced by the merger of CBS and Viacom, seriously considered cancelling the show; they finally reached an agreement to let the producers have a fourth season in order to accumulate enough episodes for minimum aftermarket syndication. However, Paramount had to cut the licence fee it demanded per episode in half; budgetary savings would be realised by shooting on high-definition video rather than on film. UPN also moved *Enterprise* to Friday nights, a ratings graveyard in which the series' falling numbers could do little harm.

In a way, things had come full circle. Just as Gene Roddenberry stepped back from running *Star Trek* when its salvation from cancellation came at the price of a poor Friday time slot and reduced budget, so Berman and Braga stepped back from running the *Enterprise* writing staff. But the executive producer they brought in, Manny Coto, creator of the short-lived *Odyssey 5* (2002) series for Showtime, was no Fred Freiberger. Many loyal Trekkers felt that he made the last season the best, rather than the worst. Under Coto, an ardent fan of the original series, *Enterprise* completely embraced its role as prequel and close cousin to *Star Trek*. His opening two-parter 'Storm Front' eliminated the Temporal Cold War altogether by having Archer and Silik go back to the 1940s to foil Vosk (Jack Gwaltney), the alien who started it all, before he could get his time-travel technology operational. In a typically utopian *Trek* touch, Silik gives his life to restore the timeline that Vosk threatened to destroy for both Suliban and humans. Subsequent episodes elucidate, among other things, the origins of the Mirror Universe, transporter technology and the smooth-foreheaded Klingons found only in the original series. Its last episodes point to the creation of the Federation and the onset of the Romulan war. 'When it was time to start the writing for Season 4, we were mostly gearing episodes towards people who knew the "Star Trek" universe,' Coto said. 'We were not worried so much about people who didn't. They were gone anyway.'[56] Braga, in retrospect, saw the wisdom of this re-orientation. 'I thought Manny Coto did a great job. One could argue that *Enterprise* might have been that from the beginning,' he said at the August 2007

143

Creation Star Trek Con in Las Vegas. 'When I was seeing what Manny was doing it was like "you know what? Maybe this should have been the show from the start." '⁵⁷

Berman and Braga, too, had wanted to recapture the basic appeal of the original starship show, *sans* the 60s' kitsch that might repel twenty-first-century viewers. But most of their callbacks to *Star Trek* sent the wrong message. To pull back from the elevated ethical discourse of Picard and Janeway, to abandon diversity in the captain's chair in favour of casting a white male North American, struck many viewers as reactionary. It's a message still conveyed in the commercials for the reruns of *Enterprise* showing on the Sci Fi Channel: 'Experience a future when the Klingons were still bad guys, the women were green, and the Captain got all the action.' More damaging than the evocation of a pre-feminist, politically incorrect mid-twentieth-century *Trek*, however, was *Enterprise*'s addition to the mythology: the demonisation of the Vulcans.

Mr Spock is such an iconic figure that neither of the first two spinoffs included a new regular or recurring Vulcan character. *Voyager*'s Tuvok continues in the dignified and honourable steps of his predecessor, even if he also acts as an overly serious wet blanket. That

Disapproving Vulcans

Vulcans believe themselves superior to humans because of their control of violent emotions has always been the case, and Vulcans can come across as arrogant. The most unpleasant Vulcan to appear on *Trek* prior to *Enterprise* is Captain Solok (Gregory Wagrowski) in *DS9*'s 'Take Me Out to the Holosuite', a longtime rival from his Academy days who lives to humiliate Sisko and dares to challenge him at his own favourite game, baseball. So the premise that Vulcans, upon making first contact with a newly warp-capable humanity, would try to slow the entry of this volatile and impulsive species into the affairs of the galaxy, makes perfect sense. As the charming flashback episode 'Carbon Creek' reveals, Vulcan surveillance of species as they first venture into space and their offers of 'guidance' once they can leave their own solar systems are the same protocols we see Picard employ in 'First Contact'.

But the Vulcans we meet in the first couple of seasons of *Enterprise* are outright racists. They complain of how bad humans smell; T'Pol must use a 'nasal numbing agent' to associate with them in the close quarters of the ship. They are also treacherous and deceitful, spying upon their Andorian foes under cover of a religious retreat. Moreover, the famed Vulcan mind-meld is considered a perverse practice and often causes a life-threatening disease that is stigmatised in the manner of HIV/AIDS. These are simply not the Vulcans any Trekker would recognise. And their obnoxiousness in turn brings out the worst in humans. A scene in 'Broken Bow' in which Archer and Tucker feast on huge steaks while condescending to the vegetarian T'Pol as she tries to cut a breadstick with a knife comes ideologically from 1951, not 2151.

To be fair, the main storyline to lead from *Enterprise* to *Star Trek* was the bridging of this gulf of misunderstanding among Vulcans, humans, Andorians and another unpleasant and quarrelsome people, the Tellarites – the four species who would come together to establish the Federation ten years after the launch of the NX-01. Archer's ability to gain (and reciprocate) the trust and friendship of T'Pol and recurring Andorian captain Shran make this alliance possible. The four allies are still squabbling in *Star Trek*'s 'Journey to Babel', so perhaps the writers

145

thought that the conflicts should be even more pronounced over a century earlier. Nevertheless, Coto saw the rehabilitation of the Vulcans as the other necessary change besides the scuttling of the Temporal Cold War. In a three-episode arc ('The Forge'/'Awakening'/'Kir'Shara') Archer's superior officer Admiral Forrest (Vaughn Armstrong) sacrifices himself to save Vulcan Ambassador Soval (Gary Graham) from a supposed terrorist bomb that is actually the work of the leader of the High Command, planted in order to discredit a dissenting religious faction, the Syrrannites. It turns out that the Syrrannites are on the right track. Vulcans have lost their way, straying from the teachings of their messiah, Surak (Bruce Gray), who taught them the discipline of logic to prevent them from letting their violent emotions destroy them. Archer and T'Pol join them and discover the original writings of Surak, long believed lost. They reveal, among other things, that mind-melding, properly conducted, is not a perversion and that those trained in its practice can cure the disease inflicted by practitioners who don't know what they're doing. That the corrupt head of the Vulcan government, V'Las (Robert Foxworth), turns out to be acting as an agent for the Romulans completes the explanation for the bizarre behaviour of *Enterprise*'s Vulcans. Soval announces the dissolution of the High Command and its baby-sitting of humans, welcoming them to the wider galaxy as equals.

146

Held Hostage

The principal areas of anxiety in the other *Trek* series are existential, worries about the vulnerability of the flesh or of consciousness, the integrity of the self or whether anything of the living survives after death. The main fear in *Enterprise* is, by contrast, situational. It is the fear of being involuntarily controlled by others. The two originary premises, of humanity held back from space by the Vulcans and of history being vulnerable to change by factions with the technology to rewrite it, touch on this theme. In addition, three out of every ten episodes have plots that involve someone being kidnapped, held

A beaten Archer, held captive by Andorians

hostage, or imprisoned, and this doesn't count a number of others that deal with characters being marooned and cut off from rescue by their shipmates. Often the captive is Jonathan Archer himself, whose captors for good measure will beat and brutalise as well. The Andorians think enough pain will make him reveal complicity in the Vulcan spying operation ('The Andorian Incident'). He is interned with innocent Suliban after being suspected of being one of the Cabal in disguise ('Detained'). He is put on a prisoner transport to a penal colony when mistaken for a smuggler in 'Canamar'. He is sentenced to life in the notorious Klingon penal colony Rura Penthe under trumped-up charges ('Judgment') and remains a wanted man after his escape, leading to his apprehension by a Tellarite bounty hunter ('Bounty'). After suffering all this abuse on the basis of misunderstandings and misidentifications, at least the brutal interrogation he suffers from the Xindi reptilians in 'Azati Prime' is the consequence of actual hostile actions taken against them.

   This anxiety may come with the territory of an American narrative post-9/11, but I cannot help but think that it also reflects the mindset of those running the show. Producing and writing still another *Trek* show had become a constricting and stressful process. The pressure

147

came from multiple directions. The CBS-Viacom merger in 1999, and particularly the ascendancy of Les Moonves in the television division, had produced a changeover in the UPN executive cohort, eliminating those who had essentially given the franchise a free pass on its poor ratings because of Paramount's bias towards its golden goose. Continued poor performance could (and did) lead to cancellation. Then there was the whole weight of four other series' worth of *Trek* history, boxing in what could be done in a prequel. And, finally, there was the adversarial relation with the group who would have usually been their strongest allies, the long-term Trekkers. Many fans, disturbed by a sharp decline in the quality of *Trek* television, pinned the blame on the two executive producers who had overseen the franchise since season five of *Voyager*: Rick Berman and Brannon Braga. Braga, particularly, felt he had started off on the wrong foot with fans when he admitted to never having watched the original series when he came to write for *TNG*, and that for that reason nothing he did would ever please them.[58] Confronted with the nitpicking about elements of *Enterprise* not lining up with what came later, he exploded in interviews that such fans were 'continuity pornographers'.[59]

148

Throughout the run of the series, 'B&B', as fans scornfully labelled the two, received unrelenting opprobrium on countless internet forums. The vitriol was so extreme that it became a subject of much entertainment media commentary on the end of the television franchise. 'There are petitions with thousands of signatures and declarations that Rick and Brannon are antichrists . . .' *IGN Film Force* reported.[60] 'Mr Berman remained remarkably sanguine for a man so frequently threatened with bodily harm on Internet message boards,' wrote *New York Times* correspondent Dave Itzkoff.[61]

Apparently feeling as beaten and bloody as poor Jonathan Archer, Berman and Braga clearly were not writing *Enterprise* out of love for the stories they were telling or of the audience members who viewed them. They were simply struggling to keep churning out *Trek* product on the franchise's failing assembly line. It's perhaps no wonder that the only episode they wrote for the last season was the one that

From the beginning *Enterprise* takes the wrong course

disavowed the shackles of *Enterprise* to give them one last chance to pen an episode of *TNG*, the pinnacle of success they had failed to duplicate in a decade of trying. Set at the end of the NX-01's ten-year mission, the series finale, 'These Are the Voyages . . .', focuses on an address given by Jonathan Archer at the signing ceremony for a human/Vulcan/Andorian/Tellarite alliance that will grow into the Federation. Archer's story, however, is presented as a historical re-creation on the holodeck, viewed by Will Riker and Deanna Troi in order to help Riker make a difficult decision presented to him in *TNG*'s episode 'The Pegasus'. Having resolved what to do, he unceremoniously ends the program just as Archer is beginning to speak. Fixated on a past recipe for success that had outlived its appeal, the last two *TNG* writer-producers to remain with the franchise finally could not propel it forward into a viable future.

149

Trek's Legacy

During a commercial break for an NFL playoff game in January 2007, forty years after *Star Trek*'s first season ran on NBC, the screen fills up with what looks like a star field, and the familiar original series theme song begins to play. The camera pulls back slightly to reveal that the star field is actually a night sky in a blizzard, seen through the windshield of a car. Cuts to the exterior of the vehicle show that it is a Hummer, speeding up a steep, snow-covered mountain road. As the theme swells to its conclusion, the camera takes a high-angle view; the car 'warps' out of sight and the caption 'Boldly go' appears. Hummer is confident that an audience far more general than that for, say, the Sci Fi Channel will recognise the visuals, the music and the 'boldly go' phrase that riff on the opening credits of this decades-old television programme.

During the anniversary year a DirectTV commercial featuring William Shatner as Captain Kirk in *Star Trek VI* and an Aleve commercial centring on Leonard Nimoy's ability to do the Vulcan salute at a *Trek* con count on the same familiarity. During this same anniversary year, a new motion picture that will reboot the franchise by featuring the early exploits of Kirk and Spock has been in pre-production at Paramount under the aegis of trendy cult writer-director J. J. Abrams. It has been announced for a May 2009 release. Meanwhile both 'remastered' and 'annotated, nested-screen' versions of original series episodes are out, the former in syndication and being readied for HD-TV and DVD release and the latter playing on cable network G4. So in this sense *Trek* is going strong.

What it isn't doing is boldly going forward, where no *Trek* has gone before. Whether the new film will spark a different direction transferable to television or whether the 700 episodes in the franchise will year by year slide deeper into the subspace of nostalgia, with only the tip that is *Star Trek* still visible, remains to be seen. Yet, to the average television viewer, humans exploring space in the future still equals *Star Trek* and one suspects that this will be as true on the centenary of *Trek*'s universe as it is now.

Notes

1 To be fair, many other scholars disagree with me and find Janeway to be an exemplary depiction of a strong yet compassionate woman. See Jan Johnson-Smith, *American Science Fiction TV* (Middletown, CT: Wesleyan University Press, 2005); Robin Roberts, *Sexual Generations: Star Trek: The Next Generation and Gender* (Urbana, IL: University of Illinois Press, 1999) and Duncan and Michèle Barrett, *Star Trek: The Human Frontier* (New York: Routledge, 2001).

2 Johnson-Smith, *American Science Fiction TV*, p. 117.

3 Letter to the author, 23 July 2007.

4 See Part I of Barrett and Barrett, Star Trek, titled 'The Starry Sea'.

5 David Alexander, Star Trek *Creator: The Authorized Biography of Gene Roddenberry* (New York: ROC/Penguin, 1994), p. 252.

6 NBC wanted the show to be as colourful as possible to foreground their 'brought to you in living colour'/Peacock network marketing campaign and to sell colour television sets for parent company RCA.

7 Jon Wagner and Jan Lundeen, *Deep Space and Sacred Time:* Star Trek *in the American Mythos* (Westport, CT: Praeger, 1998), p. 173.

8 The only exception is the casting of Hispanic-American Edward James Olmos as Adama in the new *Battlestar Galactica* (Sci Fi 2004–) (created by *Trek* alumnus Ron Moore), but that character's ethnicity is never foregrounded.

9 Barrett and Barrett, Star Trek, p. 62.

10 Thomas Richards, *The Meaning of* Star Trek (New York: Doubleday, 1997).

11 Ibid., p. 90.

12 Herbert F. Solow and Robert H. Justman, *Inside* Star Trek*: the Real Story* (New York: Pocket Books, 1997), p. 431.

13 Joel Engel, *Gene Roddenberry: The Myth and the Man Behind* Star Trek (New York: Hyperion, 1994).

14 Chris Gregory, Star Trek*: Parallel Narratives* (New York: St Martin's, 2000), p. 29.

15 Wess Roberts and Bill Ross, *Make It So: Leadership Lessons from* Star Trek: The Next Generation (New York: Pocket Books, 1995).

16 *TV Guide* Star Trek *35th Anniversary Tribute*, 22 July 2002, p. 13.

17 See Wagner and Lundeen, *Deep Space and Sacred Time*, and Lincoln Geraghty, *Living with* Star Trek*: American Culture and the* Star Trek *Universe* (London: I. B. Tauris, 2007).

18 Wagner and Lundeen, *Deep Space and Sacred Time*, p. 8.

19 See Rick Worland, 'Captain Kirk, Cold Warrior', *Journal of Popular Film and Television* vol. 16, 1988, pp. 109–17.

20 Solow and Justman, *Inside* Star Trek, p. 220.

21 See Ilsa J. Bick, 'Boys in Space: *Star Trek*, Latency, and the Neverending Story', in Taylor Harrison, Sarah Projansky, Kent A. Ono and Elyce Rae Helford (eds), *Enterprise Zones: Critical Positions on* Star Trek (Boulder, CO: Westview, 1996).

22 Wagner and Lundeen, *Deep Space and Sacred Time*, p. 130.

23 Ibid., p. 128.

24 Ingalls was so incensed at the changes Roddenberry made to endorse what his original draft had denounced that he asked to

be credited under a pseudonym, Judd Crucis.
See Alexander, Star Trek *Creator*, p. 289.

25 Engel, *Gene Roddenberry*, p. 30.

26 D. C. Fontana, 'Foreword', in Engel, *Gene Roddenberry*, p. xiii.

27 See my 'Franchise Fatigue?: The Marginalization of the Series after *The Next Generation*', in Lincoln Geraghty (ed.), *The Influence of* Star Trek *on Television, Film and Culture* (Jefferson, NC: McFarland, 2008), pp. 41–59, for a discussion of the factors that contributed to *TNG*'s success in first-run syndication. In that same volume, Dave Hipple points out that Paramount would not syndicate the original series to stations that did not agree to run *TNG* ('The Accidental Apotheosis of Gene Roddenberry, or, "I Had to Get Some Money from *Somewhere*" ', p. 36).

28 Steven F. Collins, ' "For the Greater Good": Trilateralism and Hegemony in *Star Trek: The Next Generation*', in Harrison, et al., *Enterprise Zones*, p. 141.

29 Francis Fukuyama, *The End of History and the Last Man* (New York: The Free Press, 1992).

30 Kent A. Ono, 'Domesticating Terrorism: a Neocolonial Economy of *Différance*', in Harrison et al., *Enterprise Zones*, p. 159.

31 See Collins, ' "For the Greater Good" ', and Ono, 'Domesticating Terrorism'.

32 Richards, *The Meaning of* Star Trek, p. 138.

33 Ibid., p. 75.

34 Bick, 'Boys in Space', pp. 189–210.

35 Quoted in Jeff Greenwald, *Future Perfect: How* Star Trek *Conquered Planet Earth* (New York: Penguin, 1998), p. 137. Emphasis in original.

36 Letter to the author, 13 August 2007.

37 Greenwald, *Future Perfect*, p. 64.

38 Terry J. Erdmann, with Paula M. Block, *The* Star Trek: Deep Space Nine *Companion* (New York: Pocket Books, 2000), p. 5.

39 Ibid., p. 4.

40 'Producer Ira Steven Behr Reflects on the Legacy of DEEP SPACE NINE', trekweb.com (accessed 14 July 2004), available at <http://trekweb.com/articles/2004/07/14/40f49602300c0.shtml>

41 Barrett and Barrett, Star Trek, p. 180.

42 Ibid., p. 141.

43 Bick, 'Boys in Space', p. 198.

44 Ken P., 'An Interview with Ron Moore', *IGN Film Force* (accessed 4 December 2003), available at <http://filmforce.ign.com/articles/444/444306p1.html>

45 A writer new to *Trek*, Kenneth Biller, also stayed with *Voyager* for all seven seasons. He specialised in stories that found one member of the crew at a moment of crisis, isolated either physically or psychologically from shipmates.

46 Gregory, Star Trek, p. 56. Gregory is the only previous *Trek* scholar to discuss the various writers' particular slants on writing for the programme. He differentiates Moore and Echevarria from Menosky and Braga by saying that the former are more interested in politics and the latter more interested in fantasy.

47 Rick Berman, DVD commentary, *Voyager*, Season Seven.

48 Barrett and Barrett, Star Trek, p. 128.

49 Johnson-Smith, *American Science Fiction TV*, p. 172.

50 Interview with Ron Moore, *Hypatia Kosh* (accessed 18 June 2006), available at <http://hypatia.slashcity.org/trekshack/moore.html>

51 Gregory, Star Trek, p. 101.

52 Quoted in Greenwald, *Future Perfect*, p. 197.

53 Geraghty, *Living with* Star Trek, p. 142.

54 Dave Itzkoff, 'Its Long Trek Over, The Enterprise Pulls Into Dry Dock', *New York Times*, 1 May 2005, section 2, p. 13.

55 Mark Nollinger, 'The Future of *Star Trek*', *TV Guide*, 3 March 2003, pp. 17–20.

56 Itzkoff, 'Its Long Trek Over'.

57 Brannon Braga (accessed 15 August 2007), available at <http://trekmovie.com/2007/08/12/vegascon-07-braga-reflects-on-a-life-with-trek>

58 Braga, DVD commentary, *Star Trek: The Next Generation*, Season Six.

59 'I read all these things on the Internet, these "continuity pornographers" as I like to call them, though I didn't invent the term.' Interview with Braga, 'Brannon Braga Talks Online Criticism, "Continuity Pornographers," Shorter Seasons and Burnout' (accessed 27 July 2007), available at <http://www.trekweb.com/stories.php?aid=yn9h3VM9hOqy6&mailtofriend=1>

60 Ken P., 'An Interview with Ron Moore', op. cit.

61 Itzkoff, 'Its Long Trek Over'.

Bibliography

Books and Articles

Adare, Sierra S., *'Indian' Stereotypes in TV Science Fiction: First Nations Voices Speak Out* (Austin: University of Texas Press, 2005).

Alexander, David, Star Trek *Creator: The Authorized Biography of Gene Roddenberry* (New York: ROC/Penguin, 1994).

Barrett, Michèle and Barrett, Duncan, Star Trek*: The Human Frontier* (New York: Routledge, 2001).

Bernardi, Daniel, Star Trek *and History: Race-ing Toward a White Future* (New Brunswick, NJ: Rutgers University Press, 1998).

Bick, Ilsa J., 'Boys in Space: *Star Trek*, Latency, and the Neverending Story', in Taylor Harrison, Sarah Projansky, Kent A. Ono and Elyce Rae Helford (eds), *Enterprise Zones: Critical Positions on* Star Trek (Boulder, CO: Westview, 1996), pp. 189–210.

Blair, Karin, *Meaning in* Star Trek (New York: Warner Books, 1979).

Collins, Steven F.,' "For the Greater Good": Trilateralism and Hegemony in *Star Trek: The Next Generation*', in Taylor Harrison, Sarah Projansky, Kent A. Ono and Elyce Rae Helford (eds), *Enterprise Zones: Critical Positions on* Star Trek (Boulder, CO: Westview, 1996), pp. 137–56.

Edelstein, Bill, '*Star Trek* Family Tree', *Variety*, 19 July 2006, p. A13.

Engel, Joel, *Gene Roddenberry: The Myth and the Man Behind* Star Trek (New York: Hyperion, 1994).

Erdmann, Terry J. and Block, Paula M., *The* Star Trek: Deep Space Nine *Companion* (New York: Pocket Books, 2000).

Fontana, D. C., 'Foreword', in Joel Engel, *Gene Roddenberry: The Myth and the Man Behind* Star Trek (New York: Hyperion, 1994).

Fukuyama, Francis, *The End of History and The Last Man* (New York: The Free Press, 1992).

Geraghty, Lincoln (ed.), *The Influence of* Star Trek *on Television, Film and Culture* (Jefferson, NC: McFarland, 2008).

Geraghty, Lincoln, *Living with* Star Trek*: American Culture and the* Star Trek *Universe* (London: I. B. Tauris, 2007).

Goulding, Jay, *Empire, Aliens and Conquest: a Critique of American Ideology in* Star Trek *and Other Science Fiction Adventures* (Toronto: Sisyphus Press, 1985).

Greenwald, Jeff, *Future Perfect: How* Star Trek *Conquered Planet Earth* (New York: Penguin, 1998).

Gregory, Chris, Star Trek*: Parallel Narratives* (New York: St Martin's, 2000).

Gwenllian-Jones, Sara and Pearson, Roberta E. (eds), *Cult Television* (Minneapolis: University of Minnesota Press, 2004).

Hanley, Richard, *The Metaphysics of* Star Trek (New York: Basic Books, 1997).

Hark, Ina Rae, 'Franchise Fatigue?: The Marginalization of the Series after *The Next Generation*', in Lincoln Geraghty (ed.), *The Influence of* Star Trek *on Television, Film and Culture* (Jefferson, NC: McFarland, 2007), pp. 41–59.

154

Hark, Ina Rae, '*Star Trek* and Television's Moral Universe', *Extrapolation* vol. 20, 1979, pp. 20–37.

Harrison, Taylor, Projansky, Sarah, Ono, Kent A. and Helford, Elyce Rae (eds), *Enterprise Zones: Critical Positions on Star Trek* (Boulder, CO: Westview, 1996).

Hipple, Dave, 'The Accidental Apotheosis of Gene Roddenberry, or, "I Had to Get Some Money from *Somewhere*" ', in Lincoln Geraghty (ed.), *The Influence of Star Trek on Television, Film and Culture* (Jefferson, NC: McFarland, 2008), pp. 22–40.

Itzkoff, Dave, 'Its Long Trek Over, The Enterprise Pulls Into Dry Dock', *New York Times*, 1 May 2005, section 2, p. 13.

Johnson-Smith, Jan, *American Science Fiction TV* (Middletown, CT: Wesleyan University Press, 2005).

Joyrich, Lynne, 'Feminist Enterprise: *Star Trek: The Next Generation* and the Occupation of Femininity', *Cinema Journal* vol. 35, 1996, pp. 61–84.

Krauss, Lawrence, *The Physics of* Star Trek (New York: Basic Books, 2007).

Murray, Janet, Hamlet *on the Holodeck: The Future of Narrative in Cyberspace* (Cambridge, MA: MIT Press, 1997).

Nollinger, Mark, 'The Future of *Star Trek*', *TV Guide*, 3 March 2003, pp. 17–20.

Okuda, Michael, Okuda, Denise and Mirek, Debbie, *The* Star Trek *Encyclopedia* (expanded edn) (New York: Pocket Books, 1999).

Ono, Kent A.,'Domesticating Terrorism: a Neocolonial Economy of *Différance*', in Taylor Harrison, Sarah Projansky, Kent A. Ono and Elyce Rae Helford (eds), *Enterprise Zones: Critical Positions on Star Trek* (Boulder, CO: Westview, 1996), pp. 157–85.

Penley, Constance, *NASA/TREK: Popular Science and Sex in America* (New York: Verso, 1997).

Porter, Jennifer E. and McLaren, Darcee L. (eds), Star Trek *and Sacred Ground: Explorations of* Star Trek, *Religion, and American Culture* (Albany, NY: State University of New York Press, 1999).

Rhodes, Joe, 'Ace in the Wormhole', *TV Guide*, 26 July–1 August 2003, pp. 18–21.

Richards, Thomas, *The Meaning of* Star Trek (New York: Doubleday, 1997).

Roberts, Robin, *Sexual Generations*: Star Trek: The Next Generation *and Gender* (Urbana, IL: University of Illinois Press, 1999).

Roberts, Wess and Ross, Bill, *Make It So: Leadership Lessons from* Star Trek: The Next Generation (New York: Pocket Books, 1995).

Seeley, April, ' "I Have Been, And Ever Shall Be, Your Friend": *Star Trek, The Deerslayer* and the American Romance', *Journal of Popular Culture* vol. 13, 1986, pp. 89–104.

Solow, Herbert F. and Justman, Robert H., *Inside* Star Trek: *the Real Story* (New York: Pocket Books, 1997).

Tulloch, John and Jenkins, Henry, *Science Fiction Audiences: Watching* Doctor Who *and* Star Trek (New York: Routledge, 1995).

Wagner, Jon and Lundeen, Jan, *Deep Space and Sacred Time:* Star Trek *in the American Mythos* (Westport, CT: Praeger, 1998).

Worland, Rick, 'From the New Frontier to the Final Frontier: *Star Trek* from Kennedy to Gorbachev', *Film and History* vol. 24, 1994, pp. 19–35.

Worland, Rick, 'Captain Kirk, Cold Warrior', *Journal of Popular Film and Television* vol. 16, 1988, pp. 109–17.

Websites

Chakoteya's Transcripts Site
   <www.chakoteya.net>
IGN Film Force <filmforce.ign.com>
The Internet Movie Database <imdb.com>
Sci Fi Channel <www.scifi.com>
Star Trek Official Site <www.startrek.com>
The Great Link <greatlink.org>
TrekNation <treknation.com>
Trek Today <www.trektoday.com>
TrekWeb <trekweb.com>

Credits: 100 Essential *Trek*s[*]

Star Trek

created by
Gene Rodenberry

main cast
William Shatner
Captain James T. Kirk
Leonard Nimoy
Mr Spock
DeForest Kelley
Dr McCoy
James Doohan
Scott
Walter Koenig
Chekov
Nichelle Nichols
Uhura
George Takei
Sulu

8 September 1966
The Man Trap [1.1]
directed by
Marc Daniels
written by
George Clayton Johnson

6 October 1966
The Enemy Within [1.5]
directed by
Leo Penn
written by
Richard Matheson

17 November 1966
The Menagerie Part 1 [1.11]
directed by
Marc Daniels
written by
Gene Roddenberry

24 November 1966
The Menagerie Part 2 [1.12]
directed by
Robert Butler/Marc Daniels
written by
Gene Roddenberry

15 December 1966
Balance of Terror [1.14]
directed by
Vincent McEveety
written by
Paul Schneider

9 February 1967
The Return of the Archons [1.21]
directed by
Joseph Pevney
written by
Gene Roddenberry
Boris Sobelman

16 February 1967
Space Seed [1.22]
directed by
Marc Daniels
written by
Carey Wilber
Gene L. Coon

23 February 1967
A Taste of Armageddon [1.23]
directed by
Joseph Pevney
written by
Robert Hamner
Gene L. Coon

2 March 1967
This Side of Paradise [1.24]
directed by
Ralph Senensky
written by
D. C. Fontana
Nathan Buitler [Jerry Sohl]

9 March 1967
The Devil in the Dark [1.25]
directed by
Joseph Pevney
written by
Gene L. Coon

23 March 1967
Errand of Mercy [1.26]
directed by
John Newland
written by
Gene L. Coon

6 April 1967
The City on the Edge of Forever [1.28]
directed by
Joseph Pevney
written by
Harlan Ellison

15 September 1967
Amok Time [2.1]
directed by
Joseph Pevney
written by
Theodore Sturgeon

6 October 1967
Mirror, Mirror [2.4]
directed by
Marc Daniels
written by
Jerome Bixby

20 October 1967
The Doomsday Machine [2.6]
directed by
Marc Daniels
written by
Norman Spinrad

17 November 1967
Journey to Babel [2.10]
directed by
Joseph Pevney
written by
D. C. Fontana

29 December 1967
The Trouble with Tribbles [2.15]
directed by
Joseph Pevney
written by
David Gerrold

19 January 1968
The Immunity Syndrome
[2.18]
directed by
Joseph Pevney
written by
Robert Sabaroff

Star Trek: The Next Generation

created by
Gene Roddenberry

main cast
Patrick Stewart
Captain Jean-Luc Picard
Jonathan Frakes
Commander William T. Riker
LeVar Burton
Lieutenant Geordi La Forge
Denise Crosby
Lieutenant Tasha Yar
Michael Dorn
Lieutenant Worf
Gates McFadden
Doctor Beverly Crusher
Marina Sirtis
Counselor Deanna Troi
Brent Spiner
Lt Commander Data
Wil Wheaton
Wesley Crusher

26 September 1987
Encounter at Farpoint [1.1]
directed by
Corey Allen
written by
D. C. Fontana
Gene Roddenberry

7 January 1989
Loud as a Whisper [2.5]
directed by
Larry Shaw
written by
Jacqueline Zambrano

11 February 1989
The Measure of a Man [2.9]
directed by
Robert Scheerer
written by
Melinda M. Snodgrass

6 May 1989
Q Who? [2.16]
directed by
Rob Bowman
written by
Maurice Hurley

23 September 1989
Evolution [3.1]
directed by
Winrich Kolbe
written by
Michael Piller
Michael Wagner

17 February 1990
Yesterday's Enterprise [3.15]
directed by
David Carson
written by
Ira Steven Bahr
Richard Manning
Hans Beimler
Ronald D. Moore
Trent Christopher Ganino
Eric A. Stillwell

10 March 1990
The Offspring [3.16]
directed by
Jonathan Frakes
written by
René Echevarria

16 June 1990
The Best of Both Worlds Part 1
[3.26]
directed by
Cliff Bole
written by
Michael Piller

22 September 1990
The Best of Both Worlds Part 2
[4.1]
directed by
Cliff Bole
written by
Michael Piller

26 January 1991
The Wounded [4.12]
directed by
Chip Chalmers

written by
Jeri Taylor
Stuart Charno
Sara Charno
Cy Chermak

16 February 1991
First Contact [4.15]
directed by
Cliff Bole
written by
Dennis Russell Bailey
David Bischoff
Joe Menosky
Ronald D. Moore
Michael Piller
Marc Scott Zicree

28 September 1991
Darmok [5.2]
directed by
Winrich Kolbe
written by
Joe Menosky
Philip Lazebnik

2 November 1991
Unification Part 1 [5.7]
directed by
Les Landau
written by
Jeri Taylor
Rick Berman
Michael Piller

9 November 1991
Unification Part 2 [5.8]
directed by
Cliff Bole
written by
Michael Piller
Rick Berman

21 March 1992
Cause and Effect [5.18]
directed by
Jonathan Frakes
written by
Brannon Braga

9 May 1992
I, Borg [5.23]
directed by
Robert Lederman
written by
René Echevarria

30 May 1992
The Inner Light [5.25]
directed by
Peter Lauritson
written by
Morgan Gendel
Peter Allan Fields

10 October 1992
Relics [6.4]
directed by
Alexander Singer
written by
Ronald D. Moore

12 December 1992
Chain of Command Part 1
[6.10]
directed by
Robert Scheerer
written by
Ronald D. Moore
Frank Abatemarco

19 December 1992
Chain of Command Part 2
[6.11]
directed by
Les Landau
written by
Frank Abatemarco

1 May 1993
Frame of Mind [6.21]
directed by
James L. Conway
written by
Brannon Braga

27 November 1993
Parallels [7.11]
directed by
Robert Wiemer
written by
Brannon Braga

8 January 1994
The Pegasus [7.12]
directed by
LeVar Burton
written by
Ronald D. Moore

21 May 1994
All Good Things . . . [7.25]
directed by
Winrich Kolbe

written by
Ronald D. Moore
Brannon Braga

Star Trek: Deep Space Nine

created by
Rick Berman
Michael Piller

main cast
Avery Brooks
Captain Sisko
René Auberjonois
Odo
Nicole deBoer
Lt Commander Ezri Dax
Michael Dorn
Lt Commander Worf
Terry Farrell
Lt Commander Jadzia Dax
Cirroc Lofton
Jake Sisko
Colm Meaney
Chief O'Brien
Armin Shimerman
Quark
Alexander Siddig (Siddig El-Fadil)
Doctor Bashir
Nana Visitor
Major Kira Nerys

3 January 1993
Emissary [1.1]
directed by
David Carson
written by
Michael Piller
Rick Berman

13 June 1993
Duet [1.18]
directed by
James L. Conway
written by
Peter Allan Fields
Lisa Rich
Jeanne Carrigan-Fauci

26 September 1993
The Homecoming [2.1]
directed by
Winrich Kolbe
written by
Ira Steven Behr
Jeri Taylor

3 October 1993
The Circle [2.2]
directed by
Corey Allen
written by
Peter Allan Fields

10 October 1993
The Siege [2.3]
directed by
Winrich Kolbe
written by
Michael Piller

14 November 1993
Necessary Evil [2.8]
directed by
James L. Conway
written by
Peter Allan Fields

6 February 1994
Whispers [2.14]
directed by
Les Landau
written by
Paul Robert Coyle

8 May 1994
The Wire [2.22]
directed by
Kim Friedman
written by
Robert Hewitt Wolfe

15 May 1994
Crossover [2.23]
directed by
David Livingston
written by
Peter Allan Fields
Michael Piller

12 June 1994
The Jem'Hadar [2.26]
directed by
Kim Friedman
written by
Ira Steven Behr

26 September 1994
The Search Part 1 [3.1]
directed by
Kim Friedman

written by
Ronald D. Moore
Ira Steven Behr
Robert Hewitt Wolfe

3 October 1994
The Search Part 2 [3.2]
directed by
Jonathan Frakes
written by
Ira Steven Behr
Robert Hewitt Wolfe

24 April 1995
Improbable Cause [3.20]
directed by
Avery Brooks
written by
René Echevarria
Robert Lederman
David R. Long

1 May 1995
The Die Is Cast [3.21]
directed by
David Livingston
written by
Ronald D. Moore

160

2 October 1995
The Way of the Warrior
[4.1]
directed by
James L. Conway
written by
Ira Steven Behr
Robert Hewitt Wolfe

9 October 1995
The Visitor [4.2]
directed by
David Livingston
written by
Michael Taylor

13 November 1995
Little Green Men [4.7]
directed by
James L. Conway
written by
Ira Steven Behr
Robert Hewitt Wolfe
Toni Marberry
Jack Treviño

27 January 1997
The Begotten [5.12]
directed by
Jesús Salvador Treviño
written by
René Echevarria

16 June 1997
A Call to Arms [5.26]
directed by
Allan Kroeker
written by
Ira Steven Behr
Robert Hewitt Wolfe

6 October 1997
Rocks and Shoals [6.2]
directed by
Michael Vejar
written by
Ronald D. Moore

27 October 1997
Favor the Bold [6.5]
directed by
Winrich Kolbe
written by
Ira Steven Behr
Hans Beimler

3 November 1997
Sacrifice of Angels [6.6]
directed by
Allan Kroeker
written by
Ira Steven Behr
Hans Beimler

15 April 1998
In the Pale Moonlight [6.19]
directed by
Victor Lobl
written by
Michael Taylor
Peter Allan Fields

12 May 1999
Tacking Into the Wind [7.22]
directed by
Michael Vejar
written by
Ronald D. Moore

2 June 1999
What You Leave Behind [7.25]
directed by
Allan Kroeker
written by
Ira Steven Behr
Hans Beimler

Star Trek: Voyager

created by
Rick Berman
Michael Piller
Jeri Taylor

main cast
Kate Mulgrew
Captain Kathryn Janeway
Robert Beltran
Chakotay
Roxann Dawson
B'Elanna Torres
Jennifer Lien
Kes
Robert Duncan McNeill
Tom Paris
Ethan Phillips
Neelix
Robert Picardo
The Doctor
Tim Russ
Tuvok
Jeri Ryan
Seven of Nine
Garrett Wang
Harry Kim

16 January 1995
Caretaker [1.1]
directed by
Winrich Kolbe
written by
Michael Piller
Jeri Taylor
Rick Berman

20 February 1995
Eye of the Needle [1.6]
directed by
Winrich Kolbe
written by
Bill Dial
Jeri Taylor
Hilary J. Bader

20 March 1995
Prime Factors [1.9]
directed by
Les Landau
written by
Michael Perricone
Greg Elliot
David R. George III
Eric A. Stillwell

8 May 1995
Faces [1.13]
directed by
Winrich Kolbe
written by
Kenneth Biller
Jonathan Glassner

15 May 1995
Jetrel [1.14]
directed by
Kim Friedman
written by
Jack Klein
Karen Klein
Kenneth Biller
James Thornton
Scott Nimerfro

15 January 1996
Prototype [2.13]
directed by
Les Landau
written by
Jeri Taylor

22 January 1996
Alliances [2.14]
directed by
Les Landau
written by
Jeri Taylor

6 May 1996
Tuvix [2.24]
directed by
Cliff Bole
written by
Kenneth Biller
Andrew Price
Mark Gaberman

20 May 1996
Basics Part 1 [2.26]
directed by
Winrich Kolbe
written by
Michael Piller

4 September 1996
Basics Part 2 [3.1]
directed by
Winrich Kolbe
written by
Michael Piller

6 November 1996
Future's End Part 1 [3.8]
directed by
David Livingston
written by
Brannon Braga
Joe Menosky

13 November 1996
Future's End Part 2 [3.9]
directed by
Cliff Bole
written by
Brannon Braga
Joe Menosky

9 April 1997
Before and After [3.21]
directed by
Allan Kroeker
written by
Kenneth Biller

21 May 1997
Scorpion Part 1 [3.26]
directed by
David Livingston
written by
Brannon Braga
Joe Menosky

3 September 1997
Scorpion Part 2 [4.1]
directed by
Winrich Kolbe
written by
Brannon Braga
Joe Menosky

5 November 1997
Year of Hell Part 1 [4.8]
directed by
Allan Kroeker
written by
Brannon Braga
Joe Menosky

12 November 1997
Year of Hell Part 2 [4.9]
directed by
Michael Vejar
written by
Brannon Braga
Joe Menosky

17 December 1997
Mortal Coil [4.12]
directed by
Allan Kroeker
written by
Bryan Fuller

4 March 1998
The Killing Game Part 1
[4.18]
directed by
David Livingston
written by
Brannon Braga
Joe Menosky

4 March 1998
The Killing Game Part 2
[4.19]
directed by
Victor Lobl
written by
Brannon Braga
Joe Menosky

29 April 1998
Living Witness [4.23]
directed by
Tim Russ
written by
Bryan Fuller
Brannon Braga
Joe Menosky

18 November 1998
Timeless [5.6]
directed by
LeVar Burton

161

written by
Rick Berman
Brannon Braga
Joe Menosky

25 November 1998
Infinite Regress [5.7]
directed by
David Livingston
written by
Robert J. Doherty
Jimmy Diggs

21 January 1999
Latent Image [5.11]
directed by
Michael Vejar
written by
Joe Menosky
Eileen Connors
Brannon Braga

17 February 1999
Dark Frontier Part 1 [5.15]
directed by
Cliff Bole
written by
Brannon Braga
Joe Menosky

17 February 1999
Dark Frontier Part 2 [5.16]
directed by
Terry Windell
written by
Brannon Braga
Joe Menosky

29 November 2000
Flesh and Blood Part 1 [7.9]
directed by
Michael Vejar
written by
Bryan Fuller
Jack Monaco
Raf Green

29 November 2000
Flesh and Blood Part 2 [7.10]
directed by
David Livingston
written by
Raf Green
Kenneth Biller
Bryan Fuller

17 January 2001
Shattered [7.11]
directed by
Terry Windell
written by
Mike Sussman
Michael Taylor

23 May 2001
Endgame Part 1 [7.25]
directed by
Allan Kroeker
written by
Kenneth Biller
Robert Doherty
Rick Berman
Brannon Braga

23 May 2001
Endgame Part 2 [7.26]
directed by
Allan Kroeker
written by
Kenneth Biller
Robert Doherty
Rick Berman
Brannon Braga

Star Trek: Enterprise

created by
Rick Berman
Brannon Braga

main cast
Scott Bakula
Captain Jonathan Archer
Jolene Blalock
Sub-Commander T'Pol
John Billingsley
Dr Phlox
Dominic Keating
Lieutenant Malcolm Reed
Anthony Montgomery
Ensign Travis Mayweather
Linda Park
Ensign Hoshi Sato
Connor Trinneer
Commander Charles 'Trip'
Tucker III

26 September 2001
Broken Bow (two-hour episode)
[1.1]
directed by
James L. Conway

written by
Rick Berman
Brannon Braga

31 October 2001
The Andorian Incident [1.7]
directed by
Roxann Dawson
written by
Fred Dekker
Rick Berman
Brannon Braga

23 January 2002
Dear Doctor [1.13]
directed by
James A. Contner
written by
André Jacquemetton
Maria Jacquemetton

22 May 2002
Shockwave Part 1 [1.26]
directed by
Allan Kroeker
written by
Rick Berman
Brannon Braga

18 September 2002
Shockwave Part 2 [2.1]
directed by
Allan Kroeker
written by
Rick Berman
Brannon Braga

2 October 2002
Carbon Creek [2.2]
directed by
James A. Contner
written by
Chris Black
Rick Berman
Brannon Braga
Dan O'Shannon

9 October 2002
Dead Stop [2.4]
directed by
Roxann Dawson
written by
Mike Sussman
Phyllis Strong

21 May 2003
The Expanse [2.26]
directed by
Allan Kroeker
written by
Rick Berman
Brannon Braga

5 November 2003
Twilight [3.8]
directed by
Robert Duncan McNeill
written by
Mike Sussman

19 November 2003
Similitude [3.10]
directed by
LeVar Burton
written by
Manny Coto

3 March 2004
Azati Prime [3.18]
directed by
Allan Kroeker
written by
Manny Coto
Rick Berman
Brannon Braga

12 May 2004
The Council [3.22]
directed by
David Livingston
written by
Manny Coto

8 October 2004
Storm Front Part 1 [4.1]
directed by
Allan Kroeker
written by
Manny Coto

15 October 2004
Storm Front Part 2 [4.2]
directed by
David Straiton
written by
Manny Coto

3 December 2004
Kir'Shara [4.9]
directed by
David Livingston
written by
Mike Sussman

4 February 2005
United [4.13]
directed by
David Livingston
written by
Judith Reeves-Stevens
Garfield Reeves-Stevens
Manny Coto

22 April 2005
In a Mirror, Darkly Part 1
[4.18]
directed by
James L. Conway
written by
Mike Sussman

29 April 2005
In a Mirror, Darkly Part 2
[4.19]
directed by
Marvin V. Rush
written by
Mike Sussman
Manny Coto

13 May 2005
These Are the Voyages . . .
[4.22]
directed by
Allan Kroeker
written by
Rick Berman
Brannon Braga

163

* To arrive at the figure of 100, all two-part episodes that have the same title, for example
'Unification' parts 1 and 2, count as one episode. My selection criteria took into account episodes
that establish crucial narrative and thematic memes, those that repeatedly make the 'best episode'
lists of fans and journalists, and those that are particular favourites of mine.

Index

165